CHOOSING LIBERTY IN CALIFORNIA POLICY REFORM

Examining Suicide, Discrimination
in Housing, Civil Asset Forfeiture,
and Drug Legalization

R. L. COHEN, PhD

3 Ravens Media

ISBN: 9781988557298

Published in the United States of America
by Three Ravens Media

Table of Contents

Chapter 1: Examining Suicide. 1

Chapter 2: Discrimination in Housing. 37

Chapter 3: Civil Asset Forfeiture 77

Chapter 4: Drug Legalization. 119

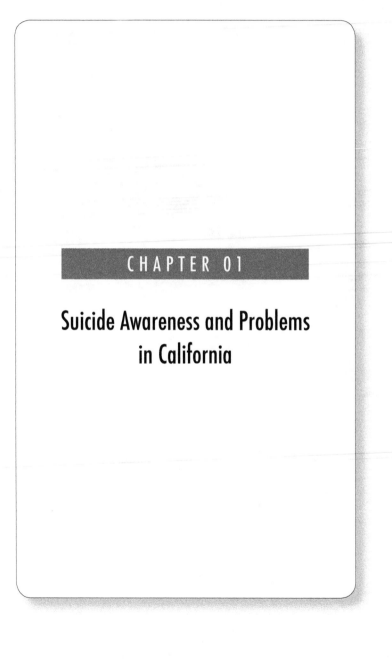

CHAPTER 01

Suicide Awareness and Problems in California

Suicide Awareness and Problems in California

Suicide is defined as the intentional taking of one's own life. Suicidal behavior is a broader term that also includes self-inflicted, potentially injurious behaviors. Suicides may be "hidden" behind tragic events, such as lethal overdoses of prescription or illegal drugs, single car collisions with a fixed object, or incidents when an individual engages in life-threatening behavior that compels a police officer to respond with deadly force. The causes of suicide are complex and varied among individuals and across ages, genders, and cultural, racial, and ethnic groups. The risk of suicide is influenced by an array of biological, psychological, social, environmental, and cultural factors. Many people who attempted or completed suicide had one or more warning signs before death. Recognition of warning signs has a greater potential for immediate prevention and intervention when those in a position to help know how to appropriately respond.

Protective factors can reduce the likelihood of suicide by counterbalancing some risk factors. These protective factors include access to effective health and mental health care, strong connections to family and community support, problem-solving skills, conflict resolution, and the nonviolent handling of disputes.

Statistics

Per data from National Center for Health Statistics, in California, during 2017–2021, the number of people who died by suicide increased from 4,323 to 4,436 annually. Between 2017 and 2018, the estimated number of suicide attempts increased from 108,075 to 112,275. Moreover, in 2017, over 1.1 million adults reported serious thoughts of suicide. California, as of 2022, is below the national average for suicide rate per 100,000 people (California = 10.7, national average = 16.4). Therefore, the growing trend should concern policymakers since the numbers are alarming. According to the California Department of Mental Health, suicide is the tenth leading cause of death in California.

Suicide risk varies in California depending on demographic factors, such as age, sex, and ethnicity. Suicide risk peaks throughout the life course, generally increasing with age. Nevertheless, it is also a leading cause of premature death. The impact of suicide on young people is a major contributor to years of life lost. Specifically, suicide is the second leading cause of death among adolescents and young adults ages 15–24 in California.

Regarding ethnicity, the suicidal rate is the highest among the White population and is reasonably higher than the state's average (15.7).[1] For American Indians and Alaska Natives, it is 12.5, while for Native Hawaiians and other Pacific Islanders, it is 10.2. The suicidal rate for Multi-Race (9.5), Black (7.6), Asian (6.7), and Latino (6.0) are below California's average. However, the growing trend is the highest among Native Hawaiians and other Pacific Islanders. It has grown from 7.3 in 2014–2016 to 10.2 in 2017–2019. Regarding sex, the suicidal rate was significantly higher for men (17.0) than women (4.0) in 2019.

Moreover, spatial variation suggests that, in 2017–2019, the northern parts of the state had higher values of suicidal rates. The highest suicidal rate in California was reported in Trinity County (37). In addition, according to the Pew Research Center (2017),[2] the highest rates of overall deaths due to suicide in California were concentrated in more rural counties.

Suicidal Risk Among the Youth

According to the Center for Disease Control and Prevention (CDC), in 2017, suicide was the second leading cause of death nationwide among young people ages 10 to 24. Of even greater concern, a 2019 United Health Foundation report cited that the teen suicide rate increased by 25% nationwide from 2016 to 2019, and California was one

[1] https://letsgethealthy.ca.gov/goals/living-well/reducing-suicide/
[2] https://www.pewresearch.org/social-trends/2017/06/22/the-demographics-of-gun-ownership/

of seven states with the most significant increases in teen suicide rates during that same period. From 2009 through 2018, the annual number of suicides of youth ages 12 to 19 in California increased from 163 to 188 (15%). In addition, self-harm—defined as self-directed behavior that deliberately results in injury—also increased in recent years. From 2009 through 2018, the annual number of reported youth self-harm incidents that led to emergency department visits or hospital stays increased from almost 10,900 to more than 16,300, an increase of 50%.

While the U.S. Census Bureau's American Community Survey 2014 to 2018 showed that counties with metropolitan areas in California had the highest number of youth suicides, the state's northern rural counties had higher suicide and self-harm rates. For example, Sierra County—a northern rural county with a population of less than 10,000—had the highest youth suicide rate in California (34 per year per 100,000 for persons ages 10 to 19). This statistic was more than nine times the statewide rate.

However, some counties with high suicide rates have experienced a relatively low total number of suicides. For example, the three counties with the highest suicide rates were northern and rural counties, with only seven youth suicides from 2009 through 2018, compared to 1,809 youth suicides statewide. The higher rate of youth suicide rates in rural counties was likely affected by the availability of mental health professionals, which are generally lower in rural counties. Studies have generally found a positive association between increased access to care and lower suicide rates. However, economic factors and sparse population density have led to shortages of mental health professionals in many rural communities, according to a report by the Rural Youth Suicide Prevention Workgroup.

In addition to variations between urban and rural areas, the rates of suicide and self-harm have also varied by gender. Data from the Office of Statewide Health Planning and Development 2009–2018 showed that males 12–19 years died by suicide at nearly three times the rate of females. Conversely, females in this same age group committed self-harm at nearly three times the rate of males. However, instances of self-harm by females increased by 64% from 2009 to 2018, more than three times the rate of self-harm by males during the same period.

Research suggests that mental health care is a critical component of suicide prevention. The Centers for Disease Control and Prevention lists barriers to accessing mental health treatment as one of the risk factors for suicide. Multiple studies have also identified positive associations between access to mental health care services—such as a higher density of psychiatrists in a given area—and reductions in suicide and factors leading to suicide. For example, a 2006 study of U.S. Census Bureau data and medical statistics found lower suicide rates in states with higher densities of psychiatrists, higher federal funding for mental health services, and lower rates of uninsured residents—correlations that the authors concluded supported the importance of clinical intervention in preventing suicide. Although identifying the exact correlation between mental health services and suicide prevention is an ongoing area of study, the current body of research indicates that increased access to mental health care reduces suicide rates.

Suicide Prevention Among the Youth

California voters recognized the importance of mental health services in suicide prevention when they voted to approve Proposition 63—known as the Mental Health Services Act (MHSA)—in 2004. The MHSA expanded services and treatment for children, adults, and seniors who suffer from or are at risk of mental illness, partly through its focus on prevention and early intervention programs. The act cited the need to address an untreated mental illness that may lead to suicide and concerns that untreated children often become unable to learn or participate in school. The MHSA imposed a 1% income tax on individuals earning more than $1 million annually and allocated about 95% of those funds to local governments. It also established the Mental Health Services Oversight and Accountability Commission (Oversight Commission) to oversee county prevention and innovation programs. In each of the last three fiscal years, the state allocated more than $1.8 billion in MHSA funds to local governments for mental health programs.

In 2018 and 2019, California had more than 1,000 school districts, 58 county offices of education, and 1,300 charter schools, known collectively as local educational agencies (LEAs). LEAs provide different types of mental health services. Some LEAs employ school counselors, school nurses, school social workers, and school psychologists, collectively referred to as mental health professionals. Because students spend a significant amount of time in school, the personnel who interact with them daily are in a prime position to recognize the warning signs of suicide and make the appropriate referrals for help. According to the National Association of School Psychologists, youth contemplating suicide frequently give warning signs of distress but are unlikely to seek help directly. Thus, training school staff to respond to youth who exhibit warning signs of suicide is imperative. Over several years, the legislature has made efforts to combat youth suicide and self-harm:

- In 2004, California passed Proposition 63, imposing a 1% tax beginning in 2005 on incomes above $1 million to expand the state's county mental health services.

- In 2007, the legislature required the Department of Health Services to establish a school health center support program in cooperation with the Department of Education.

- In 2016, the legislature required LEAs to adopt a suicide prevention policy addressing the needs of their students in grades 7–12 before the beginning of the academic year 2017–2018.

- In 2018, the legislature required California's Department of Education to identify an online suicide prevention training program to provide a grant to a county office of education to acquire and disseminate the training voluntarily to LEAs at no cost.

- In 2018, the legislature required LEAs to review their suicide prevention policies at least once every five years and update them as necessary.

- In 2019, the legislature required LEAs to adopt a suicide prevention policy for K–6 students before the beginning of the academic year 2020–2021.

Historically, state agencies have had a limited role in LEAs' suicide prevention efforts. State law charges the Department of Health Services—whose mission is to advance the health and well-being of California's diverse people and communities—with the responsibility of establishing and maintaining the state's electronic reporting system for violent deaths. Consequently, in September 2020, the governor signed a bill requiring the Department of Health Services to establish the Office of Suicide Prevention. Moreover, until recently, the role of California's Department of Education in suicide prevention was to provide specific and rather limited resources and information to schools. However, when the legislature required LEAs to adopt suicide prevention policies before the 2017–2018 academic year, it also required that the Department of Health Services develop and maintain a model policy to assist LEAs. Furthermore, in 2018, the legislature gave California's Department of Education the task of identifying one or more online programs for LEAs to use when training school staff and students on suicide prevention.

The Department of Health Care Services generally does not work directly with local educational agencies to address youth suicide prevention. Local educational agencies can receive reimbursement for some mental health care services through the state's Medicaid program: the California Medical Assistance Program (Medi-Cal). Health Care Services administers Medi-Cal through an agreement known as "the state plan" with the federal Centers for Medicare and Medicaid Services (CMS). State law requires health care services to oversee a program called the Local Education Agency Medi-Cal Billing Option Program (billing option program), where participating LEAs receive federal reimbursement for 50% of the costs of certain health-related services to Medi-Cal-eligible students under age 22. In the fiscal year 2017–2018, over 500 LEAs participated in the program and claimed nearly $134 million in federal reimbursements.

Various organizations focus on youth suicide prevention and assist schools with suicide prevention policies. For example, the Trevor Project, a national organization providing suicide prevention and crisis intervention services to LGBTQ people under age 25, cooperated with several tax-exempt organizations to create and publish a model policy for schools with procedures to assess suicide risks, along with their prevention, intervention, and responses. Another suicide prevention organization, the HEARD Alliance, a community alliance of health care professionals in the San Francisco Bay area, works to increase collaboration among primary care, mental health care, and education professionals to enhance the community's ability to prevent suicide in adolescents and young adults, among other things.

In addition, LEAs sometimes partner with community-based organizations to provide mental health and counseling services to their student populations. Some LEAs also partner with community-based organizations to provide services on-site, including mental health assessments, individual counseling sessions, and crisis counseling. LEAs may also refer at-risk students to off-site community-based mental health services.

Suicidal Problems Among Veterans

One societal group severely exposed to suicidal problems is Veterans. A Veteran is "a person who served in the active military, naval, or air service, and who was discharged or released there from under conditions other than dishonorable"[3] (National Veteran Suicide Prevention Annual Report, 2019, np).

---

[3] https://www.ssa.gov/OP_Home/ comp2/D-USC-38.html

Due to the character of their service, this societal group can suffer from traumatic brain injury (TBI) or post-traumatic stress disorder. These disorders have been significantly increasing among older Veterans (75 years and older) and thus sustained the highest number of TBIs among any age group. Major depression is the most frequent psychiatric disorder post-TBI, affecting nearly 30% of post-injury patients in the first year alone and may play a role in older Veterans having the greatest number of suicides among all Veteran age groups.

In 2013, the U.S. Department of Veteran Affairs released a study covering suicides from 1999 to 2010, which showed that roughly 22 Veterans died by suicide per day, or one every 65 minutes. Some sources have suggested that this rate may be undercounting suicides. A 2013 analysis found a suicide rate among Veterans of approximately 30 per 100,000 per year, compared with the civilian rate of 14 per 100,000. However, the comparison was not adjusted for age and sex. According to a 2016 report published by the U.S. Department of Veterans Affairs that analyzed 55 million Veterans' records from 1979 to 2014, an average of 20 Veterans died from suicide daily (Office of Mental Health and Suicide Prevention, U.S. Department of Veterans Affairs, 2021).

Nationally, the total number of suicides differs by age group: 31% of these suicides were by Veterans 49 and younger, while 69% were by Veterans 50 and older. As with suicides in general, Veteran suicide is primarily related to males—approximately 97% in the states reporting gender. Moreover, a significant disparity in suicidal ideation and completion rates has been identified among marginalized groups such as LGBTQ military members. Suicidal ideation was two to three times greater in LGBTQ active-duty and Veteran service members, with transgender Veterans committing suicide at double the rates of their cisgender peers.

California has more Veterans than any other state—approximately 8% of all U.S. Veterans live there. California has an estimated 1,578,509 Veteran communities, more than four times the average number of Veterans in other U.S. states. California is also home to the largest Selected Reserve population, with 57,031 members, including the Army National Guard, Air National Guard, Army Reserve, Air Force Reserve, Navy Reserve, Marine Corps Reserve, and Coast Guard Reserve. Although exact numbers are unavailable, approximately half the California's National Guard are prior-enlisted and, as Veterans and citizen-soldiers, warrant support from the California Association of Veteran Service Agencies and the Californians who relied on their service.

The most up-to-date information on Veteran suicide rates was reported in the Veteran Association's 2020 National Veteran Suicide Prevention Annual Report between 2005 and 2018. Nationally, there was not a significant increase in Veteran suicide rates. In contrast, in California, the U.S. Department of Veteran Affairs 2018 State Data Sheet showed a decrease from 640 Veteran suicides (representing 15.3% of all suicides and 1.2% of all Veteran deaths) to 526 Veteran suicides per 100,000 population. Despite the decline, the absolute numbers are still reasonably high considering the total numbers since California is home to the biggest Veteran community in the country.

According to the California Association of Veteran Service Agencies, the greatest percentage of Veteran suicides (54%) occurs among the 65–85+ age group, compared to 16% of suicides of non-Veterans in that age group. This result is partly because of the older age structure of Veterans but still skews higher among them. Notably, 97% of suicides among Veterans were male, and 79% were White. Similar to the US, California's highest Veteran suicide rate is in rural areas, with 46% reporting gun ownership compared to 28% in the suburbs and 19% in urban areas. Another potential cause of having a higher suicidal rate in rural than urban areas may be long distances to health care facilities and trauma centers, with higher rates of opioid overdoses.

Regarding suicide mechanisms, firearms were used in 66% of Veteran suicides, twice as often as non-Veterans (33%). This data from the California Association of Veteran Service Agencies points to the necessity of expanding our public health dialogue about the management of "access to means" (of lethality) and improved provider and community education on this potentially life-saving topic.

However, while active-duty service members confront the suicidal problem, it is also related to non-activated

Guard/Reserve. There are high Guard and Reserve component suicide rates, with 32.2 per 100,000 for never-federally-activated former National Guard members as a serious cause for concern.[4] Because former National Guard and Reserve members are former service members who do not have Veteran federal legal status due to their type of service, they typically do not have access to Veteran benefits and services under current laws and regulations. Many California National Guard members summoned for state service by the governor to manage natural disasters have extensive service periods but do not qualify for federal Veteran benefits.

The suicidal problem can also affect relatives of Veterans. According to a 2019 report from the Department of Defense, 186 military family members died by suicide—122 among active-duty families, 29 among Reserve families, and 35 among National Guard families. Moreover, 17 spouse suicides were the service members themselves, with firearms as the primary mechanism of death among all spouses, differing from the general population.

Suicide Prevention Among Veterans

The high suicide rate among U.S. military Veterans has been an ongoing phenomenon and raised concerns in the 1950s when the first suicide prevention center in the

---

[4] https://www.mentalhealth.va.gov/docs/data-sheets/2019/2019_National_Veteran_Suicide_ Prevention_Annual_Report_508.pdf

US was opened. During the mid-1990s, a paradigm shift in addressing Veteran suicide occurred by developing a national strategy that included several congressional resolutions.

More advancements were made in 2007 with the Joshua Omvig Veterans Suicide Prevention Act, supporting the creation of a comprehensive program to reduce the incidence of suicide among Veterans. The act required the Secretary of the U.S. Department of Veterans Affairs (VA) to implement a comprehensive Veteran suicide prevention program. Components include staff education, mental health assessments as part of overall health assessments, a suicide prevention coordinator at each VA medical facility, research efforts, 24-hour mental health care, a toll-free crisis line, and outreach to and education for Veterans and their families. In the summer of 2009, the VA added a one-to-one "chat service" for Veterans who prefer to reach out for assistance using the internet.

In 2010, the National Action Alliance for Suicide Prevention was created; in 2012, the National Strategy for Suicide Prevention was revised. With Obama's administration, suicide prevention strategies for Veterans expanded to find and obtain mental health resources easier for Veterans, retain and recruit mental health professionals, and make the government programs more accountable to the people they serve.

In 2012, President Barack Obama signed Executive Order (EO) 13625, "Improving Access to Mental Health

Services for Veterans, Service Members, and Military Families." The EO called on the cooperation of the Department of Defense, the VA, and local communities to improve their mental health care services for military service members, especially during their transition into civilian life. This order was specifically written to expand Veteran suicide prevention and drug abuse efforts, demanding the Veteran Crisis Line's capacity be expanded by 50% by the end of 2012 and the Veterans Health Administration (VHA) to connect any Veteran in a mental health crisis to a mental health professional or trained mental health worker within 24 hours of contacting the Veteran Crisis Line.

In 2015, the Clay Hunt Veterans' Suicide Prevention Act was enacted. It required the Secretary of Veterans Affairs to organize an annual third-party evaluation of the VA's mental health care and suicide prevention programs, mandating website updates at least once every 90 days about mental health care services, offering educational incentives for psychiatrists who commit to serving in the VHA, collaborating with non-profit mental health organizations to prevent Veteran suicide, and extending Veterans' eligibility for VA hospital care, medical services, and nursing home care. However, the limitations of this act are quite restrictive. Veterans can only access extended eligibility if they were discharged or released from active duty between 2009 and 2011 and did not enroll in care during the five years following their discharge.

In 2019, the U.S. president Donald Trump signed an EO called the PREVENTS Initiative to counter Veteran suicide. The initiative aimed to equip state and local governments with the resources necessary to identify and intervene in scenarios where U.S. Veterans may be at risk of suicide. In the past, the Veteran's Administration and other federal agencies relied upon the Veteran to self-identify when needing help. $73.1 billion was secured for Veteran health services, including $18.6 billion for mental health services of the $73.1 billion in funding.

In November 2019, the House of Representatives discussed a potential program that would grant local organizations supporting Veterans whom the Department of Veterans Affairs had possibly overlooked. The motivation behind targeting this demographic of overlooked Veterans was that statistically, an estimated 14 of 20 Veterans and current service members who die from suicide daily were not in regular communication with the VA. This proposal, pushed by the VA, was for a test program to last three years. However, this idea languished in Congress despite some bipartisan support.

Several state and national programs and policies have targeted suicide prevention among Veterans. For instance, the VA designed the Reach Vet program to identify Veterans at risk of suicide who would have otherwise been missed. The Reach Vet program applies statistical algorithms to clinical data to produce a monthly list of Veterans with the highest probability of dying by suicide

(Reger et al., 2019). A coordinator at each VA facility receives the list of at-risk patients and alerts the Veterans' health care providers.

Moreover, the VA provides the Caring Contacts program. Caring contacts are brief, personal, nondemanding follow-up messages sent to patients after they receive care. These messages have been linked to decreased suicide attempts (Motto & Bostrom, 2001). The VA now sends follow-up letters to Veterans who receive care at a VA facility or call the Veterans Crisis Line and choose to identify themselves to the call responder (VA, 2020). VA researchers are testing the approach with other patient populations, including those seen in VA emergency departments (Landes et al., 2019).

In addition to tracking data, the VA and VHA partner with the Department of Health and Human Services Substance Abuse and Mental Health Services Administration on the National Strategy for Preventing Veteran Suicide. In this 10-year suicide prevention strategy, they outlined a framework for state and local entities to prioritize efforts to end Veteran suicide. Under this strategy, two operational plans were developed: Suicide Prevention 2.0 (SP 2.0) and the Suicide Prevention Now (Now) initiatives.

SP 2.0 includes a community-based intervention for suicide prevention (CBI-SP) approach and a clinical approach focusing on the broad dissemination of evidence-based psychotherapies. SP 2.0 CBI-SP reaches Veterans inside and outside the VA's system by embracing cross-agency collaborations and community partnerships. SP 2.0 CBI-SP migrates three initiatives into a comprehensive approach to community-based suicide prevention, addressing needs at state and local community levels: 1) the state-based coalition and collaboration building model (i.e., the Governor's Challenge), 2) the Veterans Integrated Service Network (VISN)-based community coalition and collaboration building model (e.g., VISN-wide community suicide prevention pilot programs), and 3) the Veteran-to-Veteran coalition-building model (i.e., Together With Veterans). For state-level prevention, the VA and the Substance Abuse and Mental Health Service Administration (SAMHSA) expanded the Governor's Challenge to Prevent Suicide Among Service Members, Veterans, and Their Families. The VA, SAMHSA, and state-level policymakers partner with local leaders to implement a comprehensive suicide prevention plan through these efforts. For local community action through interstate efforts, the VA is expanding community-based efforts across all VISNs with community engagement and partnerships for suicide prevention focused on community coalition-building combined with targeted outreach and education.

Finally, the VA is expanding community-based efforts through rural Veteran-to-Veteran approaches through the Together With Veterans program, partnering with the VA's Office of Rural Health program to focus on building partnerships with rural Veterans and their communities to implement community-based suicide prevention. Five evidence-based strategies support local planning efforts designed for community-wide implementation to increase awareness and knowledge about Veteran suicide and improve community response to local Veterans' needs.

Across all three approaches to CBI-SP, there are three overarching priority areas:

1. identifying Service members, Veterans, and their families and screening for suicide risk;
2. promoting connectedness and improving care transitions; and
3. increasing lethal means safety and safety planning.

SP 2.0 clinical efforts are focused on increased access to evidence-based psychotherapies for suicide prevention. To that end, the VA's Suicide Prevention Program has partnered with the VA's national Clinical Resource Hub leadership team to foster national telehealth capability to provide these treatments outlined in the CPG. The VA is currently hiring over 100 clinicians to provide these treatments across 140 healthcare systems. In addition to SP 2.0 community and clinical efforts, the SP 2.0 model is built upon a foundation of mental health and suicide prevention staffing to ensure Veterans have access to a full continuum of mental health services.

The minimal outpatient mental health staffing ratio includes 7.72 outpatient mental health full-time employee equivalent (FTEE) staff per 1,000 Veterans in outpatient mental health and a national minimum benchmark for suicide prevention staffing at 0.1 suicide prevention coordinator/case manager FTEE per 1,000 Veterans enrolled at a facility. Currently, suicide prevention staffing models are being revised to help best inform staffing needs with an expansion of suicide prevention efforts in the VA.

The other important initiative is the Now initiative, which aims to initiate quick deployment of interventions deemed to most efficiently impact Veterans at high risk for suicide within one year. The five areas of focus include the following:

1. lethal means safety;
2. suicide prevention in medical populations;
3. outreach to and understanding of prior VHA users;
4. suicide prevention program enhancements (e.g., REACH VET and Safety Planning in the Emergency Departments expansion);
5. paid media.

Over the past years, several advancements have been accomplished through Now, including mandatory training requirements of all VHA providers in lethal-means safety, expanded partnerships with the National Shooting Sports Foundation and American Foundation for Suicide Prevention for publishing a lethal-means safety toolkit, piloting efforts to re-engage prior VHA users, reaching all five REACH VET performance metrics nationally, increased safety planning in the emergency department from a baseline of 35% to 86%, and significant expansion of paid media campaigns.

Suicide Prevention Institutions and Initiatives in California

Federal and state governments and California's counties all play a role in the governance and oversight of public mental health services. The federal Center for Medicare and Medicaid Services establishes and enforces minimum standards that states can expand. For example, states may experiment with new or innovative services and delivery models with federal approval (Mental Health America, n.d.). Within state and federal parameters, California counties have "broad discretion" in how they fund and provide mental health services to target populations, including determining budgets and priorities (Arnquist & Harbage, 2013).

At the state level, several institutions are responsible for mental health policy in California. For instance, the **California Behavioral Health Planning Council** advocates for children with serious emotional disturbance and adults with serious mental illness, evaluating the public behavioral health system, participating in statewide planning, and advising the legislature on priority issues. The **Department of Health Care Services** administers Medi-Cal, the MHSA, and the Community

Mental Health Block Grant. Contracts with local mental health plans to provide specialty mental health services to children and adults in Medi-Cal. The **Mental Health Services Oversight and Accountability Commission** oversees the Mental Health Services Act programs and is responsible for developing strategies to reduce stigma, possibly advising the governor and the legislature on mental health policy.

The Behavioral Health Advisory Boards review and evaluate community mental health needs, services, and facilities at the county level and advise behavioral health directors. The **County Behavioral Health Departments** arrange for and deliver behavioral health services for Medi-Cal beneficiaries with serious mental illness, substance use disorders, and other safety-net populations. The **County Boards of Supervisors** oversee county departments and programs with input from the Behavioral Health Advisory Boards and appropriate funding for behavioral health services.

Selected Programs

Medi-Cal, covering nearly 13 million Californians with low incomes, provides mental health services through managed care plans (MCPs), the fee-for-service (FFS) system, and county mental health plans (MHPs), which provide specialty mental health services. The state requires MCPs and MHPs to coordinate services. However, there are often "serious disconnects" between these two providers

(Lewis & Coursolle, 2017). Counties provide additional mental health services through the Mental Health Services Act and local "safety-net" programs.

MCPs are the "dominant mode of service delivery" in MediCal (Tatar & Chambers, 2019). The state contracts with MCPs to deliver services in exchange for a monthly premium, or "capitation" payment, for each Medi-Cal beneficiary. In FFSs, Medi-Cal providers are reimbursed for each service or visit (Tatar et al., 2016). MCPs must provide certain mental health services to adults age 21 or older with mild to moderate mental health conditions. MCPs also must provide certain mental health services to children and youth under age 21 regardless of the severity of the impairment. Mental health services available through MCPs are also available through the FFS system.

Mental Health Services Act (MHSA) Programs. In 2004, California voters approved Proposition 63, creating a 1% surtax on personal income above $1 million to provide increased funding for mental health services. The purpose of the MHSA is to expand mental health services and supports to children and adults, focusing on innovation and prevention. The MHSA has established parameters for how the funds are spent. Most (95%) of MHSA funding goes directly to counties with some flexibility in using these funds. The remainder (5%) is reserved for state-level MHSA administration.

Striving for Zero: California's Strategic Plan for Suicide Prevention 2020–2025. This strategy has four main aims: 1) to establish suicide prevention infrastructure, 2) to minimize risks for suicidal behavior by promoting safe environments, resiliency, and connectedness, 3) to increase early identification of suicide risk and connection to services based on risk, and 4) to improve suicide-related services and supports.

On **the county level**, the state contracts with county MHPs to provide SMHSs, as authorized by the federal Medicaid 1915(b) waiver. Medi-Cal beneficiaries who meet medical necessity criteria are eligible for SMHS, with more stringent criteria applied to adults age 21 and older. For children and youth under 21, SMHSs are provided through the Early and Periodic Screening, Diagnostic and Treatment benefit. Children and youth are eligible for mental health services, including SMHS, when those services are necessary to correct or ameliorate an emotional or mental health condition.

Shortcomings

Federal and state policy changes have increased the number of people receiving services through Medi-Cal. The most significant change was the expansion of Medi-Cal in 2014 to many adults with low incomes who were previously ineligible. Hence, many Californians with particular mental health needs became eligible for county-provided SMHS.

However, the number of Medi-Cal beneficiaries receiving SMHS has not kept pace with overall enrolment in the program. While Medi-Cal enrolment is up by nearly 88% between 2008–2009 and 2020–2021 (projected), the number of Medi-Cal beneficiaries receiving SMHS is projected to rise by less than 50% during this period.

Recent Developments

The 2020–2021 budget recently signed by Gov. Gavin Newsom includes $2 million to fund measures outlined in the report, aiming to help local governments, educators, industry, health care providers, community organizations, and everyday Californians do a better job detecting and responding to suicide risk. Key to those prevention efforts is establishing state-level leadership to push for long-term reductions in suicide death and suicidal behavior. Therefore, Assembly Bill 2112 created an Office of Suicide Prevention within the California Department of Public Health.

Free Market Solutions: A Discussion

Over the past decade, several economists, journalists, sociologists, and mental health practitioners have posited that the increases in mental illness and distress are due to neoliberal economic policies and ideologies. Neoliberalism encourages individualism, which has decreased emphasis on the need for community and social connection for fulfillment. Since individualism is viewed as a desirable moral characteristic, asking for help, especially financially, is frowned upon.

Additionally, economic and social policies created in line with neoliberal ideology favor individualism, materialism, and competitiveness, which are incompatible with human needs such as social connection and community, leading to anxiety and depression (James, 2008). Furthermore, through poor access to mental healthcare due to the for-profit healthcare system and the medicalization of emotional distress due to the rise of biological psychiatry, how we treat mental illness in the US has also contributed to rising rates of anxiety and depression (Case & Deaton, 2020; Cohen, 2016). Due to neoliberal practices in the US since the 1980s, the decreased funding for social programs and welfare reform has contributed to increased diagnosis of mental illness as traditional welfare programs have shifted to only provide for people with medical or psychiatric illnesses (Hansen et al., 2014).

Moreover, in 1996, President Clinton signed the Personal Responsibility and Work Opportunity Act, putting stricter requirements on traditional welfare, such as a five-year limit for benefits, stricter eligibility, and work participation requirements (Hansen et al., 2014). Changing these policies did not decrease the need for financial support, so many people who needed assistance applied for Social Security income (SSI) instead (Hansen et al., 2014). This result can be seen through the dramatic increases in Social Security recipients since 1996, reaching a 50%–100% growth in the number of young adult beneficiaries by 2000 (Hansen et al., 2014).

However, these benefits can only be received with a medical or psychiatric diagnosis, with a psychiatric diagnosis being the largest diagnostic category (Hansen et al., 2014). This limitation is likely a significant driver for the increase in mental illness diagnoses and medication consumption, as taking psychiatric medication is frequently required for SSI benefits (Hansen et al., 2014). It may also lead providers to medicalize distress due to the consequences of poverty to give their patients eligibility for financial assistance (Hansen et al., 2014).

Studies have shown an increase in mental distress among unemployed participants enrolled in the program by 6.75% due to anxieties from the threat of losing essential income due to minor infringements and pressure to apply for a high volume of jobs (Wickham et al., 2020).

Neoliberal capitalism not only increases distress and contributes to rising rates of psychiatric disorders but also dictates how we diagnose and treat mental distress. The for-profit healthcare system and the pharmaceutical industry's influence on how psychiatry is practiced have been guided by profitability in recent years (Davies, 2017). Psychiatry moved to a biological approach, and its scope expanded, which worked to medicalize distress, shift cultural perception about what is "normal" and "abnormal," and strengthen the idea that failure to succeed in the dominant society is an individual problem that must be corrected by individual treatment (Cohen, 2016).

The pharmaceutical industry has worked to link the *Diagnostic and Statistical Manual of Mental Disorders* (DSM) to biological abnormalities and began to promote biological psychiatry by investing in public health campaigns and financing nearly all clinical trials into psychiatric medication (Davies, 2017). Treating psychiatric illness through medication is also more cost-effective as a clinician can now see three to four people during a 1 hr session and is therefore favored by profit-driven health insurance companies (Davies, 2017). Some of these changes were driven by profits but also worked to legitimize the neoliberal social order (Cohen, 2016; Davies, 2017).

The DSM increased the number of mental disorders from 182 to 265, medicalizing subjective experiences that had previously fallen outside of the professional domain (Cohen, 2016). The DSM's applications went beyond psychiatry, being used in clinical settings and courts, research, insurance reimbursement, managed care, and patient self-diagnosis (Cohen, 2016).

Outside of psychiatric institutions, neoliberal health and wellness discourses allow for a more subtle social control that governs people's behavior at a distance and encourages people to self-monitor for symptoms of mental illness that can be diagnosed and corrected to maximize personal productivity (Cohen, 2016; Esposito & Perez, 2014). As psychiatric discourse expanded, so have the number of symptoms that constitute mental illness leading to the medicalization of normal responses to life's stressors under neoliberal capitalism (Cohen, 2016; Moncrieff, 2008).

Privatizing U.S. healthcare has caused costs to rise much higher than healthcare costs in other countries, yet health outcomes and life expectancy are worse (Case & Deaton, 2020). Health care is considered a commodity rather than a social right. Hence, there is disproportionate access to healthcare, so the unemployed or underemployed do not have access to healthcare and therefore have worse outcomes (Nkansah-Amankra et al., 2013)

References

Arnquist, S., & Harbage, P. (2013). *A complex case: Public mental health delivery and financing in California* [Report]. California Health Care Foundation. https://www.chcf.org/wp-content/uploads/2017/12/PDF-ComplexCaseMentalHealth.pdf

Case, A., & Deaton, A. (2020). *Deaths of despair and the future of capitalism*. Princeton University Press.

Cohen, B. M. Z. (2016). *Psychiatric hegemony: A Marxist theory of mental illness*. Palgrave Macmillan.

Davies, J. (Ed.). (2017). *The sedated society: The causes and harms of our psychiatric drug epidemic*. Palgrave Macmillan.

Esposito, L., & Perez, F. M. (2014). Neoliberalism and the commodification of mental health. *Humanity & Society, 38*(4), 414–442. https://doi.org/10.1177/0160597614544958

Hansen, H., Bourgois, P., & Drucker, E. (2014). Pathologizing poverty: New forms of diagnosis, disability, and structural stigma under welfare reform. *Social Science & Medicine, 103*, 76–83. https://doi.org/10.1016/j.socscimed.2013.06.033

James, O. (2008). *The selfish capitalist: Origins of affluenza*. Vermilion.

Lewis, K., & Coursolle, A. (2017). *Mental health services in Medi-Cal* [Issue brief]. National Health Law Program. https://

healthlaw.org/wp-content/uploads/2017/01/1.12.17-MentalHealthServicesMediCal.pdf

Moncrieff, J. (2008). Neoliberalism and biopsychiatry: A marriage of convenience. In C. Cohen & S. Timimi (Eds.), *Liberatory psychiatry: Philosophy, politics and mental health* (pp. 235–256). Cambridge University Press. https://doi.org/10.1017/cbo9780511543678.013

Motto, J. A., & Bostrom, A. G. (2001). A randomized controlled trial of postcrisis suicide prevention. *Psychiatric Services*, *52*(6), 828–833. https://doi.org/10.1176/appi.ps.52.6.828

Nkansah-Amankra, S., Agbanu, S. K., & Miller, R. J. (2013). Disparities in health, poverty, incarceration, and social justice among racial groups in the United States: A critical review of evidence of close links with neoliberalism. *International Journal of Health Services*, *43*(2), 217–240. https://doi.org/10.2190/hs.43.2.c

Office of Mental Health and Suicide Prevention, U.S. Department of Veterans Affairs. (2021). *2021 National Veteran Suicide Prevention Annual Report.* https://www.mentalhealth.va.gov/docs/data-sheets/2021/2021-National-Veteran-Suicide-Prevention-Annual-Report-FINAL-9-8-21.pdf

Reger, G. M., McClure, M. L., Ruskin, D., Carter, S. P., & Reger, M. A. (2019). Integrating predictive modeling into mental health care: An example in suicide prevention. *Psychiatric Services*, *70*(1), 71–74. https://doi.org/10.1176/appi.ps.201800242

Tatar, M., & Chambers, R. (2019). *Medi-Cal and behavioral health services* [Fact sheet]. California Health Care Foundation. https://www.chcf.org/wp-content/uploads/2019/02/MediCalExplainedBehavioralHealth.pdf

Tatar, M., Paradise, J., & Garfield, R. (2016, March 2). *Medi-Cal managed care: An overview and key issues*. Kaiser Family Foundation. https://www.kff.org/medicaid/issue-brief/medi-cal-managed-care-an-overview-and-key-issues/

Wickham, S., Bentley, L., Rose, T., Whitehead, M., Taylor-Robinson, D., & Barr, B. (2020). Effects on mental health of a UK welfare reform, Universal Credit: A longitudinal controlled study. *The Lancet Public Health*, 5(3), e157–e164. https://doi.org/10.1016/s2468-2667(20)30026-8

CHAPTER 02

The Ugly Truth About
Civil Asset Forfeiture:
We Are All Usual Suspects in the Eyes
of Law Enforcement

The Ugly Truth About Civil Asset Forfeiture: We Are All Usual Suspects in the Eyes of Law Enforcement

Private property rights are extremely important to Americans because we would not have a private life protected from government infringements if we did not have property rights. Most Americans would be outraged if law enforcement officers could seize their well-deserved property without charging them with a crime. Fortunately, such unlawful administrative sanctions are not permitted in the US! After all, life, liberty, and pursuit of happiness cannot be guaranteed without private property rights.

While this is the prevailing belief among Americans, the truth may shock many of us. Throughout the US, police and prosecutors can confiscate cash, a home, or any private property suspected of being associated with a crime. Moreover, public authorities do not need to charge or associate private property owners with a crime because the subject of the suspected crime is the property, not the owner. You can question how an entity without a will can be held responsible for any crime. However, law enforcement forces believe it is possible and does not need any court process or an actual criminal charge to have that conviction. Do you think what I have said is absurd and devoid of legal basis? Unfortunately, you are mistaken. Civil asset forfeiture laws fully equip law enforcement forces with these powers throughout the US.

You may think that law enforcement forces use civil asset forfeiture as an emergency and exceptional method to rationalize this mind-boggling unlawfulness. However, the facts still frustrate us. Law enforcement forces forfeit billions of dollars worth of property each year at the local, state, and federal levels. As a result, asset forfeiture is a frequent rather than exceptional legal practice. It has evolved into a standard procedure rather than an emergency.

I know you are becoming more and more confused about the subject. You say, "To effectively fight organized crime, civil asset forfeiture must be used to prevent the trafficking of money and goods of great value." Some newspaper headlines you read may have imposed this opinion on you, but the statistics again point to the contrary. According to research by the Institute for Justice (IJ), the average monetary value of the total forfeiture in 21 states is $1,276 (Knepper et al., 2020). In some states, this average is even lower. However, it is impossible to know the exact figures for all states as asset forfeiture data is often extremely difficult to access. As we see, asset forfeiture is hardly used to catch kingpins or prevent large money-laundering operations.

Asset forfeiture victims are often too disadvantaged to seek their rights through legal means. Even if you object to civil asset forfeiture by exercising your legal rights, the average fee you will pay to a lawyer for a lawsuit is $3,000 (Texas Appleseed, 2017). Therefore, consent to unlawful treatment is more economically meaningful than hiring a lawyer to seek your rights. Of course, you may want to defend your rights without a consultant. However, the complexity of the bureaucratic procedures you must go through often leaves you needing a lawyer, so you must fight to prove your innocence even though no charges have been brought legally. If you do not file a lawsuit to prove your innocence, your forfeited property or cash is automatically left for the use of law enforcement agencies. It is no surprise that statistics show that asset forfeiture remains uncontested by 75% (Knepper et al., 2020). Civil asset forfeiture laws are based on the assumption that citizens are suspects until they prove their innocence. Therefore, it is difficult to fight or win a legal fight against these laws.

Although citizens are vulnerable to civil asset forfeiture laws, it is an extremely lucrative legal practice for law enforcement because forfeiting agencies use these proceeds as a part of their budget. According to the Policing for Profit report by the IJ, $68.8 billion of property has been confiscated since 2000 (Knepper et al., 2020). This figure has been calculated based on available data. It is also important to remember that data is not accessible or publicly disclosed. While $23 billion of these proceeds were collected under state laws, $46 billion were collected under federal laws (Knepper et al., 2020). Through the federal equitable sharing program, state law enforcement agencies can forfeit property in collaboration with federal law enforcement using federal law. Up to 80% of the proceedings resulting from this cooperation can be left to state and local law enforcement agencies (Drug Policy Alliance, 2019). The importance of income from forfeiture for law enforcement agencies becomes even more apparent when considering that 70% of the property forfeited in 2018 was cash or convertible goods (Knepper et al., 2020).

Another reason civil asset forfeiture laws endanger the rule of law in the US is the cash flow set aside for law enforcement purposes. Law enforcement officers can forfeit property without showing evidence beyond "reasonable doubt." In many states, a mere "preponderance of the evidence" is found sufficient to prove the case for asset forfeiture in court if the owner can contest the official claims (Drug Policy Alliance, 2019; Stahl, 1992). Moreover, the proceeds obtained from civil asset forfeiture are turned over to law enforcement agencies to be used for law enforcement purposes. If a citizen successfully reclaims forfeited property through a court order after overcoming all legal obstacles, law enforcement is not liable for the court decision. Even if citizens win the case against the law enforcement officers, they cannot recover the costs of the lawsuit from the law enforcement agency.

Accurate information on how these proceeds are used is difficult to obtain. As a result, asset forfeiture laws may present law enforcement agencies with negative incentives. At the least, the proceeds received through a non-transparent legal process are spent opaquely. Civil asset forfeitures are mostly processed through administrative decisions, another sign that asset forfeiture methods are not transparent. As a result, police or prosecutors usually forfeit the property acting unilaterally and without meaningful recourse to a judicial decision or court process (Knepper et al., 2020).

At the federal level and in many states, agents do not even need the court for administrative forfeiture. It is sufficient for the agency or prosecutor to notify the owner of the government's intention to forfeit the property. While the owner can take the forfeit intent to court within the statutory time window, this timeframe is both short and costly to file a lawsuit against the government. The property is automatically forfeited if the owner does not go to court.

According to the IJ's data, 78% of the forfeitures processed by the Department of Justice between 2000 and 2019 were administrative. Only 6% of the forfeitures had a judicial process initiated, while 16% were criminal forfeitures. Likewise, 96% of Treasury forfeitures were administrative (Knepper et al., 2020).

However, the procedures of criminal forfeitures significantly differ from civil asset forfeitures. Forfeiting agencies or prosecutors must charge the owners with a property-related crime and show concrete evidence beyond a reasonable doubt. In contrast to administrative forfeiture, criminal forfeiture must be heard by an impartial judge. These statistical data are the result of malign incentives created by administrative forfeiture.

It is challenging to find data on forfeiture types at the state level, whether criminal or civil. It is also unclear whether any judicial process has been begun for civil forfeitures. Data collected by the IJ from Arizona, Connecticut, and Oregon are as follows. In Arizona, 93% of forfeits were civil. In Connecticut, 71% of forfeits were civil, and in Oregon, 74% of forfeitures were civil (Knepper et al., 2020).

In this context, we can briefly examine California's forfeiture profile. At the state level, California forfeited $440 million in property between 2002 and 2018, according to available data. Between 2000 and 2019, California law enforcement agencies received $1.3 billion in proceeds from forfeited properties from federal equitable sharing. However, since 2016, in California, agencies can only receive proceeds of forfeited property worth over $40,000 from federal equitable sharing. For this reason, post-2016 federal level forfeitures partially decreased (Knepper et al., 2020).

In uncontested forfeiture cases, California forfeiting agencies can only present a "prima facie case" to forfeit the property worth less than $40,000. A prima facie case is a rebuttable presumption presumed right until proven wrong. So, it is akin to probable cause and not a strong defense for the rights of the owner or the defendant. In uncontested cases, the properties can be forfeited fairly easily on the part of the forfeiting agency, with no conviction of the third-party owner. However, a weak conviction provision is required if the owner contests the forfeiture. Nevertheless, as we know, the financial and bureaucratic burden of the case can easily discourage the owners from defending their rights.

Despite some improvements to its forfeiture law in 2016, California offers little detail on forfeited properties. It does not disclose the individual value of the forfeited properties or the type of property. Moreover, California does not disclose the type of forfeitures. Therefore, it is unclear whether forfeited properties are civil or criminal. As a result, in civil forfeitures, no data exist on whether a judicial process is running. Although 76% of forfeiture proceeds go to law enforcement, California does not report how proceeds are spent (Knepper et al., 2020).

Thus, we do not have data to evaluate whether forfeiture funds are used in the fight against crime, as assumed by many Californians.

In the US, the seizure and forfeiture of property can be processed in a non-serious manner in terms of civil asset forfeiture. The problem is that civil forfeiture laws are designed against property rights, and the records of forfeitures are far from transparent. Using such arbitrary power by the federal government and other forfeiting agencies and prosecutors is largely rationalized by the war on crime. Forfeitures are generally used in white-collar crimes and the war on drugs. Law enforcement forces can fight these crimes with broad and opaque powers that can be called arbitrary because these crimes point to some critical junctures in American history.

However, it is doubtful how successful these arbitrary forfeitures are with the crimes brought forward. The first reason for this suspicion is that there is no clear record of the crime associated with the forfeitures. In particular, there are no records where we can evaluate the effectiveness of civil-administrative forfeiture. In most cases, these records are largely closed to the public. Second, some studies show that there is no significant change in crime rates in states where civil forfeiture is reformed according to the principles of the rule of law.

Excuses for Civil Forfeiture: The Road to Hell Is Paved With Good Intentions

A legal practice contrary to the rule of law, such as civil forfeiture, needs strong rationalization. Forfeiture supporters impose the indispensability of forfeiture on citizens in the written and oral media almost daily. We can group civil forfeiture supporter claims into two categories. The first claim is that civil forfeiture is essential to confiscate criminals' profits.

Indeed, criminal investigations are insufficient in the fight against crime. When the currency traffic of the suspects is interrupted, it prevents the perpetration of the crime and its attractiveness (Ingraham, 2017). This method is an extraordinary and aggressive attitude toward crime because it ignores the presumption of innocence, the principle that "everyone is innocent until proven guilty." Moreover, the citizen must prove that the property is not related to the alleged crime.

Such primitive methods of combating crime have not been seen in modern Western civilization since the 17th century. At least, most people think so. The most important reason such primitive practices have survived is our belief that we live in extraordinary times. "Extraordinary" almost always prevails over common sense. The crimes related to "extraordinary" is organized crime organizations, such as drug cartels, activities related to terrorism, and white-collar crimes such as money laundering and Ponzi schemes.

Recently, forfeiting property has become common in crimes related to white-collar settings. However, especially alleged crimes such as drugs and terrorism can provide forfeiture to be accepted easily and unquestioningly by the public. Scant publicly available documents can prove the success of forfeitures in the fight against crime. However, forfeiture advocates cannot stop talking about the success of forfeiture in the fight against drugs in the media.

In the second category, some argue that civil forfeiture proceeds could help to combat crime and compensate crime victims (Office of the Inspector General, U.S. Department of Justice, 2021). Specifically, supporting anti-drug or community programs financed by forfeiture will increase social cohesion. In short, the bad guys' money is taken from them and transferred to the good guys. As a result, civil forfeiture laws, which are in legal limbo, serve a social purpose. It is usually not public how the forfeiture proceeds are allocated. However, in some states where this information is available, the financial resources are transferred to social programs at a level that does not justify civil forfeiture (Knepper et al., 2020).

An important way to tell whether civil forfeiture is being used to deter organized crime or the illegal international movement of money is to look at the average value of forfeited properties and currencies. As explained above, this average is just over $1,000 at the state level. According to recent data, half the Department of Justice's (DOJ) forfeitures were approximately $12,000. The same data was roughly $7,300 for the Treasury (Knepper et al., 2020).

The federal government is adept at reporting and highlighting major events associated with organized crime. However, publicly available data show that forfeitures of great value are the exception rather than the rule. There is almost no public data to legitimize the fight against organized crime. On the contrary, undisclosed data strengthen our suspicions about civil forfeitures.

The DOJ, Treasury, and DHS have extensive databases of forfeited properties at the federal level, yet they do not retain information on which assets are associated with convictions or criminal investigations. If we do not know what crimes individual forfeitures are involved in, how can we know whether forfeitures are effective in the fight against crime? Although such information is only found in Pennsylvania, it is not specified whether the conviction in question is related to civil or criminal forfeiture (McDonald & Carpenter, 2021).

One of the strategic goals of the DOJ's Asset Forfeiture Program (AFP) is to "Prevent Crime, Protect the Rights of the American People, and Enforce Federal Law." However, in the audits conducted by the Office of the Inspector General (OIG) every year, no conclusion can be reached regarding the effectiveness of the AFP. The OIG's 2017 report on the subject states (Office of the Inspector General, U.S. Department of Justice, 2017):

> There is no applicable Asset Forfeiture Program (AFP) performance measures. No performance measures are indicated because the AFP's operations are performed by its participants. The AFP is considered to be an enabling/administrative activity where resources are spread across agencies in accordance with full program costing guidance. (p. 9)

The OIG has stated that it cannot assess the issue as no records monitor the effectiveness of asset forfeiture. The

OIG's 2020 report recommended that metrics to measure the effectiveness of forfeitures should be developed, and a separate unit responsible for these records should be established, but this recommendation has not yet been met (Office of the Inspector General, U.S. Department of Justice, 2021).

As explained above, forfeiting agencies do little to prove the role of forfeitures in the fight against crime. With the statements they make from time to time, forfeiting agencies expect citizens to believe that forfeitures are effective in the fight against crime. They do not see any objection in the operation of direct government intervention to the right to property, one of the most basic human rights, independent of civil control.

This attitude toward property rights is fundamentally against the check and balance system on which the U.S. Constitution is built. It is an important human rights violation that a fundamental human right changes hands without complying with constitutional principles, especially in civil asset forfeitures with no judicial process. The purpose, scope, and application of restrictions on human rights cannot be independent of judicial review (Harvard Law Review, 2018). This principle is the basic principle that separates civilized and uncivilized societies.

Fortunately, in 2015, New Mexico passed legislation that greatly increased judicial review on forfeiture and limited the privileged rights of forfeiting agencies. Under this law, effective July 1, 2015, all civil asset forfeitures were abolished in New Mexico, and forfeiting agencies were prohibited from transferring property worth less than $50,000 to the federal government under the equitable sharing program. Thus, all forfeitures were subject to judicial review, and the incentives that caused law enforcement to forfeit low-value assets were eliminated.

During the discussion on forfeiture legislation, the spokespersons of the law enforcement agencies claimed that the law in question would create a great weakness in the fight against crime and deprive law enforcement of the necessary resources. Fortunately, the field research of the IJ conducted in New Mexico in 2020 examined whether a weakness emerged in the fight against crime after 2015. According to the results, the removal of civil asset forfeitures did not cause any detectable change in crime rates that could be attributed to the forfeiture reforms in New Mexico (Knepper et al., 2020).

The research focused on two important variables before and after 2015. The first was whether there was an increase in crime rates between these periods. If law enforcement was weakened by reform, a jump in crime rates would be expected. The second was whether there was a serious decrease in police arrests. Thus, an efficiency analysis could be made by comparing the change in crime rates with the police's fight against crime in the context of arrest rates. In addition, the reliability of the data obtained was tested by comparing the crime trends of New Mexico with Colorado and Texas. This study showed no significant change in crime rates or criminal arrests compared to the period before 2015. In addition, no change in crime trends after 2015 was observed between the crime trends in neighboring states and New Mexico (Knepper et al., 2020).

Grading the States and Federal Government

IJ's research has developed a grading system to measure human rights violations of federal and state forfeiture practices, evaluating states and the federal government in the context of three issues: financial incentives, innocent owner protections, and the standard of proof. Most, sometimes all, of the forfeit proceeds are allocated as an additional budget to the forfeiting agency or prosecutor. Forfeitures allow law enforcement to self-finance outside the normal legislative budget.

Before the Philadelphia District Attorney's Office and Police Department shut down its self-funding program, forfeit proceeds comprised 20% of the DA's budget. This ratio reflected the average across the US. The 2019 research conducted by Brian Kelly within the scope of thousands of forfeiting agencies showed a positive correlation between the budget inadequacies of law enforcement and forfeiture revenues. Considering that 80% to 100% of the forfeiture proceeds in 32 states were left to law enforcement, the chances of law enforcement agencies putting the proceeds before justices also increased (Kelly,

2019). Law enforcement agencies only have no financial incentives for forfeiture in New Mexico, Missouri, D.C., Michigan, North Carolina, and Maine.

The second element, innocent owner protection, is a complete legal disgrace. In civil forfeitures, two separate cases are conducted if the litigation process starts. The first is the civil lawsuit filed by the owner of the forfeited property to prove his innocence (in most cases, the burden of proof is placed on the owner), and the other is the criminal lawsuit on the link of the property to the crime. The defendant must prove that he did not know that the property, whose relationship with the crime has not been finalized, was used in the alleged crime and that he did not consent to its use in the alleged crime. Since the case is not against the person but the property, although there is no charge against the person and the property's connection with the crime has not yet been proven, the property owner must prove the innocence of the alleged crime. In 13 states, the governments try to prove the owner's guilt of the alleged crime by waiting to be proven in the criminal court (Knepper et al., 2020).

In criminal forfeitures, only one criminal case is begun, and it is the person who is charged, not the property. The property is forfeited if a causal relationship is established between the property and the crime. However, in criminal cases, the connection between the crime, person, and property is clear, and forfeiting property depends on proving the crime beyond probable cause. Nevertheless, this proof is not the case in civil forfeiture.

Assume that the person could not prove that he did not know about the connection of his property to the alleged crime, and the case was settled against him. Since the civil case is not directly related to the criminal case, he may lose his property regardless of the outcome of the criminal case. Reinstatement remains subject to a lengthy legal battle, which is the case in 29 states and under federal law. However, the government is responsible for proving the crime in 13 states and D.C. In the remaining eight states, it depends on the type of the forfeited property (Knepper et al., 2020).

When a person dares to bring a civil suit unfairly filed against him, his proof of innocence is based on a different standard of proof in each state. Therefore, it is important in which state his property is seized under civil forfeiture laws. The standard of proof defines how convincing the government's evidence must be to prevail in court. In civil forfeiture cases, the preponderance of the evidence is mostly enough for the government to win the case, so circumstantial evidence, with no direct connection to the alleged crime, is enough to deprive the owner of his property. Only in three states, New Mexico, Nebraska, and North Carolina, was civil forfeiture abolished, so the government needs a criminal case to seize property. In Maine, probable cause is enough to seize the property. In other states, the law requires a weak to strong conviction provision (Knepper et al., 2020).

However, as previously mentioned, for the conviction provision to be applied, the property owner must contest the forfeit and file a civil lawsuit. Even if the property owner is found not guilty in the civil case, a third party can be subject to the rule of the conviction provision in the criminal case, and the property can still be forfeited. All of this may seem overwhelming to you. Since forfeits are often uncontested, properties are seized without a conviction provision. In this respect, a weak or strong conviction provision does not effectively protect the property owner from unfair forfeits.

Based on the three criteria outlined above, the IJ's Policing for Profit Report awards states and the federal government an overall score: 34 states and federal governments earned Ds. Massachusetts had the lowest grade of F. Nine states, including California, received Cs in the reform process. You can view the entire list in the table below.

Civil Forfeiture Law Grades Rank

Table 1 - *Civil Forfeiture Law Grades Rank*

State	Grade	State	Grade
New Mexico	A	Montana	D-
Wisconsin	A-	Iowa	D-
North Carolina	B+	Pennsylvania	D-
D.C.	B+	Utah	D-
Maryland	B+	Michigan	D-
Missouri	B+	Ohio	D-
Maine	B+	Kentucky	D-
Connecticut	C	Arkansas	D-
California	C	New Jersey	D-
Florida	C	North Dakota	D-
Oregon	C	Virginia	D-
Colorado	C	Alabama	D-
Nebraska	C	Arizona	D-
New York	C	Nevada	D-
Mississippi	C-	Tennessee	D-
Vermont	C-	Wyoming	D-
Alaska	D+	Delaware	D-
Louisiana	D+	Georgia	D-
Texas	D+	Hawaii	D-
Minnesota	D	Idaho	D-
New Hampshire	D	Kansas	D-
Indiana	D	Oklahoma	D-
Illinois	D-	South Dakota	D-
Rhode Island	D-	West Virginia	D-
South Carolina	D-	Federal Government	D-
Washington	D-	Massachusetts	F

Resource: Institute for Justice, Policing for Profit, 2020, p. 42.

Looking at the above table, we argue that most states suspended constitutional rights in the context of civil forfeiture. The most important reason is that states enact the federal civil forfeiture laws by imitating federal forfeiture laws, which often violate constitutional guarantees and property rights. In contrast, reform efforts simply develop in the context of the campaigns of some non-governmental organizations and are basically organized as a local resistance.

While success has been achieved in some states, the scope of the reforms remains limited. The most important reform will undoubtedly be repealing the federal civil forfeiture law. Other states would quickly follow this example. The most important reason the reforms made in the states have not yielded significant results is that the federal forfeiting agencies promote the federal equitable sharing program to break the restrictions and regulations introduced for civil forfeiture in the states.

Studies on the subject often state that the financial and procedural regulations enforced by the DOJ to protect the constitutional rights of citizens in the forfeiting process are usually not followed, or the negligence of the local forfeiting agencies is not audited. A comprehensive study of how the federal equity sharing program could be abused at the state and local levels was conducted in California. The research of the Drug Policy Alliance covering the years 2006–2013 revealed that the civil forfeiture practices used, especially in the fight against drugs, were not audited in California (Drug Policy Alliance, 2015).

Civil Asset Forfeiture in California

Before the war on drugs began, civil forfeiture was a rarely used legal tool, and its scope was extremely limited. The Comprehensive Drug Abuse Prevention and Control Act of 1970 expanded the fight against drugs. Initially used by law enforcement to seize drugs and drug equipment, civil forfeiture was quickly used to seize other assets, especially currency. Assets and currencies traceable to drug transactions became subject to civil forfeiture in 1978. In 1984, real property and, in 1986, cars, boats, businesses, houses, and land were included in the list of things that can be seized under civil forfeiture laws (Drug Policy Alliance, 2015).

Moreover, the DOJ's Assets Forfeiture Fund, established in 1984, prevents the transfer of forfeiture proceeds to the Treasury's General Fund. With this new fund, the federal equitable sharing program has been initiated, making it possible for state law enforcement to participate in joint investigations with federal agencies. Thus, state law enforcement officers retain a sizable portion of the forfeit proceeds after they carry out the property seizures, called adoptive forfeiture, within the framework of federal laws. Hence, forfeitures not allowed under state laws have proceeded under federal laws, and the state government is prevented from auditing these forfeitures. While the proceeds of the DOJ's Asset Forfeiture Fund were $93.7 million in 1986, this figure reached $8.2 billion in 2017 (Drug Policy Alliance, 2015).

Since 2016, assets worth less than $50,000 in California cannot be subject to adoptive forfeiture. Thus, California law enforcement's share of federal equitable sharing is lower than most other states. However, these adaptive forfeitures have continued to increase over the years in California. Since 2016, no studies have investigated how many of California law enforcement's adoptive confiscations are regulatory-compliant. Nor does the DOJ have an audit program open to the public concerning state or local forfeiting agencies. In any case, the information about how many forfeitures are civil or criminal is not publicly available in California. However, the Drug Policy Alliance study (2006–2013) is informative.

The Drug Policy Alliance examined the federal forfeiture revenues of more than 300 cities, counties, and state law enforcement agencies between 2006 and 2013 to understand how civil asset forfeiture was practiced in California. Then, each city's federal forfeiture proceeds were divided by that city's population, and the federal forfeiture income per capita was obtained. Thus, the top ten cities with the highest federal forfeiture income per capita (Vernon, Irwindale, Beverly Hills, El Centro, La Verne, South Gate, Pomona, Baldwin Park, Calexico, Gardena, and West Covina) were found. Interestingly, eight of the top ten cities were in Los Angeles County (Drug Policy Alliance, 2015).

Table 2

Cities with highest federal forfeiture

City	County	Population	Forfeiture Revenue	Per Capita Forfeiture Revenue	Per Capita Forteiture Revenue per year
Vernon	LA	112	$986,275	$8806	$1,101.00
Irwindale	LA	1,422	$802,856	$565	$71.00
Beverly Hills	LA	34,109	$7,321,005	$215	$27.00
El Centro	Imperial	42,598	$4,555,024	$107	$13.00
La Verne	LA	31,063	$3,014,653	$97	$12.00
South Gate	LA	94,396	$7,622,071	$81	$10.00
Pomona	LA	149,058	$11,688,230	$80	$10.00
Baldwin Park	LA	75,390	$4,925,018	$65	$8.00
Calexico	Imperial	38,572	$2,496.740	$65	$8.00
Gardena	LA	58,829	$3,759,425	$64	$8.00
West Covina	LA	106,098	$6,181,838	$58	$7.00
Source :	Equitable Sharing Agreement and Cerification reports	and Census data			
Note :	The small first nations community of Los Coyotes (pop.288)	is ranked 9th for per capita forfeiture. However, it was not included	because it only reported DOJ forfeiture revenue in 2 years since FY 2000	and the total amount of money involved is quite small ($21,451).	

Source: Above the Law: An Investigation of Civil Asset Forfeiture in California, Drug Policy Alliance, 2015, p. 22.

This study primarily explores the extent to which the law enforcement agencies in this ten-city list comply with the regulations set by the DOJ, which clearly declared that civil asset forfeiture "is not designed to be, and should not be used as, an alternative funding source for state and local law enforcement" (Drug Policy Alliance, 2015, p. 6). To achieve this goal, the DOJ mandated that state law enforcement agents follow certain regulations, including not making revenue estimations and not supplanting to protect the integrity of federal equity sharing. Supplanting is cutting the city's police budget by the forfeiture revenue of that year. In other words, the legislator is aware that forfeiture can easily be used for purposes other than fighting crime.

The nine cities on this list have systematically violated the DOJ's regulations. Among the various regulatory violations, these cities' annual forfeiture revenue estimation is the most interesting, which amounts to millions of dollars in some cities. The annual forfeiture estimation is proof that these cities view their forfeiture income as a continuation of their normal budget, which the DOJ expressly prohibits (Drug Policy Alliance, 2015).

As an extreme example, one of Pomona's forfeiture expectations was $3.1 million. Although Pomona had a forfeiture balance of $526,079 in its budget at the beginning of the 2006 fiscal year, Pomona estimated that it would spend $1,772,275 in forfeiture funds that same year. Interestingly, Pomona achieved over $1,400,000 in forfeiture revenues that year, closing the forfeiture fund deficit in the budget. The research revealed similar things happened in 2005, 2007, 2009, 2010, 2014, and 2015. However, the Pomona Police Department refused the request for a meeting on the subject (Drug Policy Alliance, 2015).

Budget cuts suspected of supplanting were also found in the study. The Vernon Police Department's 2010 forfeiture budget and the following year's budget cut were quite close. Similar examples were given in the research from the budgets of the Irwindale and La Verne Police Departments. However, it is very difficult to prove budget cuts intended to supplant.

The research also encountered widespread reporting and audit deficiencies related to federal civil forfeiture in the nine cities. When cities spent over $500,000 in federal grants annually, their spending was audited as part of a "single audit." Apart from this federal audit, forfeiture revenues were included in the municipal budget and reported on the relevant forms of the DOJ, and ultimately revenues and appropriations were itemized in the comprehensive annual financial report (Drug Policy Alliance, 2015).

However, the study found significant inconsistencies among the reports of many cities. In addition, some cities avoided audits. For example, $1.25 million in forfeiture revenues collected by the police were not included in the Vernon municipal budget in 2010, and the comprehensive annual financial report did not account for these forfeiture revenues and expenditures. Moreover, a $420,000 difference was found between the forfeiture revenues shown in the West Covina municipal budget and the revenues reported to DOJ in the 2012 fiscal year. The difference between forfeiture expenditures presented to the California DOJ in the same year and forfeiture expenditures presented in the municipality budget was also approximately $400,000 (Drug Policy Alliance, 2015).

Besides audit and reporting problems, the forfeiting agencies examined do not fill in the forms they need to fill in the property seizure or do not retain the filled forms. Previous studies have shown that police officers occasionally do not give the owners a document about the property they have seized. Without this receipt, it is usually not possible for the property owner to contest the agency's forfeiture (Kelly, 2019).

For example, the city of La Verne has largely delayed filling out the DAG-71 form required for each forfeiture. Indeed, the DAG-71 form was filled or kept for only one of six forfeitures between 2008 and 2013. A similar omission was found in South Gate. It is notable in the research that many cities refused to provide information about DAG-71 forms during the study (Drug Policy Alliance, 2015). You may acquire a general idea about the breaches of regulations by examining the table below.

Table 3 *Breaches of Federal Forfeiture Regulations*

City	Anticipating forfeiture revenue	Possible supplanting	Failure to perform Single Audit of forfeiture expenditures	Large discrepancies between forfeiture data in different fiscal records	Failure to retain records associated with federal asset forfeiture (see note 2 below)
Vermon	×	×		×	
Inwindale		×	×		
Beverly Hills	1	×			
La Verne	×	×		×	×
South Gate	×				×
Pomona	×		×	×	
Baldwin Park	×		×	×	
Gardena	×		×		
West Covina	×			×	
Notes	1) Beverly Hills included future forfeiture revenue in its municipal budget one year only and it was roughly equivalent to the amount of interest it earned on its forfeiture reserves the previous year.			2) The extent of this problem is not entirely known as only Gardena and La Verna responded to Public Records Act requests for DAG-71 forms.	

Source: Above the Law: An Investigation of Civil Asset Forfeiture in California, Drug Policy Alliance, 2015, p. 26.

One of the most striking findings of the research is that despite the thousands of documents examined, no record exists of how civil asset forfeitures help society in the fight against drugs. None of the forfeitures have been associated with a specific crime, and the results of the cases against the forfeitures are undisclosed. Moreover, despite the many irregular practices obtained in the study, there is no trace of any sanctions that the DOJ may have applied against the aforementioned forfeiting agencies. The DOJ stated that it could not make a statement on the subject because the DOJ has not followed the sanctions forced against forfeiting agencies (U.S. Department of Justice, Asset Forfeiture Program, 2008).

Whose Properties Are Forfeited in California?

According to the American Civil Liberties Union (ACLU) of California's Civil Asset Forfeiture Policy Brief, 85% of law enforcement officers who receive civil forfeiture proceeds in California serve People of Color. Half of California's Drug Enforcement Administration (DEA) seizures involve Latino names. In California, counties with above-average seizures have a lower average income than the California median. The chart below shows that People of Color's properties are forfeited more often than other groups based on official statistics (ACLU of California, 2016).

Figure 4

Equitable Sharing Payments

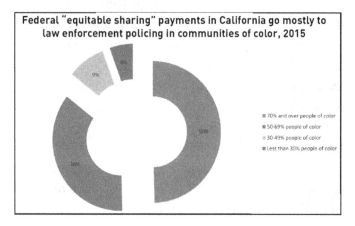

Note. ACLU, Policy Brief, Civil Asset Forfeiture, Profiting From California's Most Vulnerable, 2016, p. 6.

According to the 2016 report published by East Bay Community Law Center, "Stopped, Fined, Arrested, Racial Bias in Policing and Traffic Courts in California," "there are dramatic racial and socioeconomic disparities in driver's license suspensions and arrests related to unpaid traffic fines and fees" (Lawyers' Committee for Civil Rights of the San Francisco Bay Area, 2016, p. 1). As data from the California Department of Motor Vehicles and the U.S. Census shows, African Americans and Latinos are five times more likely to have their driver's license suspended than the state average. African American and Latino motorists are also much more likely to have their licenses suspended than White motorists (Lawyers' Committee for Civil Rights of the San Francisco Bay Area, 2016).

Two important reasons exist for this racial disparity. The first is simply that the police stop and search for People of Color more than Whites. The second reason is that People of Color have more difficulty paying traffic fines and infraction citations. Failure to pay traffic fines has consequences, including jail time. The seriousness of the problem can be better understood when considering that traffic courts are also likely to have a bias against People of Color. Thus, when People of Color violate traffic rules, they are more likely to be caught and punished than Whites (Lawyers' Committee for Civil Rights of the San Francisco Bay Area et al., 2016).

People of Color are more affected by civil or federal forfeiture than other socioeconomic groups. People with Latino surnames were included in 49% of the 364 forfeitures performed by the DEA (February–May 2015). Half of the proceeds from the federal sharing equitable program go to police departments in counties where 70% of the population is People of Color. If the share of People of Color in the population is more than 50%, the rate of proceeds going to the police departments rises to 85% (ACLU of California, 2016). The table below shows the highest forfeiture rates per capita in 2014.

Table 5 *Per Capita Seizure Rates*

California Counties with Highest Per Capita Seizure Rates, 2014			
County	2014 per capita seizure rate	Median Household Income, 2010-2014 (in 2014 dollars)	Persons living in poverty, %
Trinity	$17.06	$36,862	19.9%
Imperial	$7.46	$41,772	23.6%
Inyo	$4.50	$45,625	14.0%
Los Angeles	$3.21	$55,870	18.7%
San Bernardino	$2.81	$54,100	20.4%
Humboldt	$2.73	$42,153	21.0%
Glenn	$2.40	$40,106	17.1%
Nevada	$2.02	$56,949	11.4%
San Mateo	$1.95	$91.421	7.5%
Shasta	$1.94	$44,556	14.7%
Sources: Department of Justice, U.S. Census Bureau (2014 population projections), ACLU analysis.			

Source: ACLU, Policy Brief, Civil Asset Forfeiture, Profiting From California's Most Vulnerable, 2016, p. 7.

The information given above indicates that law enforcement acts with bias against People of Color in California. However, the ACLU's research emphasizes another important issue. People of Color living in counties whose household income is below the state average are more likely to carry cash than other income groups.

Half of all African American and Latino households are unbanked or underbanked (ACLU of California, 2016). The fact that these people carry cash does not mean they engage in illegal activities. Rather, these people work jobs with no income security, and their earnings are barely enough to meet their daily needs. You rarely need a bank account if you do not have the income to invest or save. Furthermore, banks are unwilling to give you a credit card if your credit scores are not good enough.

Unfortunately, the vulnerability of these people in California makes them a favorite of forfeiting agencies. These people always carry cash with them, are marginalized by society, are incapable of protecting their legal rights, and can easily fit into the criminal profile. No wonder the average forfeiture proceeds of law enforcement agencies is approximately $1,000. These people cannot afford to carry larger monetary sums on them.

Personal Stories of the Victims of Forfeiture

The stories told here are based on legal documents and interviews with victims. The stories are examples of how the practice of civil forfeiture can turn into an arbitrary discretion that cannot be easily controlled.

Janitorial Business Owner

In 2014, a businesswoman driving her car on the San Diego I-5 freeway was pulled over by the LA County

Sheriff's Deputies. The police, who told the driver they stopped her because she was driving suspiciously, got the driver out of the car and into the back of the police car. The officers found $18,000 when they searched the car. Although the woman showed the police the documents proving that the money was withdrawn from the company account and would be distributed to the employees as wages, the police did not find the woman's answer convincing. After the officers seized the businesswoman's money and her car, they abandoned her at a closed Santa Clarita police station. The woman got her money and car back due to her lawsuit. However, the lawsuit took two years (ACLU of California, 2016).

Taco Truck Owner

Near Lancaster, a taco truck owner was pulled over by the police and asked if he was carrying cash with him. There were no drugs in the car, and his job was legal. The taco truck owner did not hide the $10,000 he was carrying from the police. However, the police seized the taco truck owner's money while the taco truck owner was not charged with or arrested for any crime. The taco truck owner filed a lawsuit against forfeiture and won. However, the Los Angeles County Sheriff's Department reported that the money had been transferred to the federal fund and could not return the money. At this point, the taco truck owner could not sue the U.S. government to get his money back because the process of suing the U.S. government was expensive and dangerous for many reasons (ACLU of California, 2016).

Computer Repair Shop Owner

In June 2010, the police raided the computer repair shop that Frank Ranelli had run for 20 years and seized 130 computers. Some computers were for sale, while others were waiting to be repaired. Police claimed that Ranelli was selling stolen computers, citing evidence of an informer. However, when Ranelli showed he had the computers by taking the official procedures, they dropped the charges against him. Nevertheless, Ranelli could not retrieve his confiscated computers after years of trying.

Conclusion

The essential difference between a civilized and an uncivilized government is that the government's monopoly on the use of force is subject to judicial review within the context of individual liberty. Our basic individual rights, such as the right to property, are innate rights we can claim against the government through judicial processes. We do not have to prove anything to any authority to have these rights. However, if the political authority wants to limit our individual rights or take away our property, it should do this within the framework of the universal rules of law. Otherwise, political authority's use of power over individuals' losses is legitimized.

The studies examined in this chapter show that even if we accept the success of civil asset forfeiture in the fight against crime, there is no possibility of keeping this practice under democratic-civic control. Law enforcement forces have such arbitrary discretional powers that they cannot stay uncorrupted. If you are closing your eyes to this lawlessness because you think that civil asset forfeiture will prevent usual suspects from committing crimes, you are making a big mistake. If the law cannot protect the most vulnerable, no one is safe in that society. On the contrary, by turning a blind eye to this unlawfulness, you are encouraging law enforcement and public officials to abuse their power. What needs to be done is not to reform civil asset forfeiture but abolish it altogether. The unlimited power that civil forfeiture gives law enforcement to citizens cannot be kept under control or used for good intentions.

The only type of forfeiture compatible with the rule of law is criminal forfeiture. However, legal consultancy should be provided to the defendant in criminal forfeiture to ensure sufficient legal protection against the prosecutor. Moreover, studies show that much information about criminal forfeitures is not publicly available and is not adequately audited by the DOJ. Although criminal forfeitures are conducted through judicial review, they must be thoroughly audited and reported to determine the success of criminal forfeitures in the fight against crime and to be subject to democratic oversight. Otherwise, forfeitures will continue to erode all of the ideas and beliefs on which the U.S. Constitution is based.

References

American Civil Liberties Union of California. (2016). *Civil asset forfeiture: Profiting from California's most vulnerable* [Report]. https://www.aclunc.org/docs/aclu_california_civil_asset_forfeiture_report.pdf

Drug Policy Alliance. (2015, April 20). *Above the law: An investigation of civil asset forfeiture in California.* https://drugpolicy.org/resource/above-law-investigation-civil-asset-forfeiture-california

Drug Policy Alliance. (2019, January 3). *Civil asset forfeiture.* https://drugpolicy.org/resource/civil-asset-forfeiture

Harvard Law Review. (2018). How crime pays: The unconstitutionality of modern civil asset forfeiture as a tool of criminal law enforcement. *Harvard Law Review, 131*(8), 2387–2408.

Ingraham, C. (2017, July 19). Jeff Sessions's defense of civil asset forfeiture, annotated. *The Washington Post.* https://www.washingtonpost.com/news/wonk/wp/2017/07/19/jeff-sessions-defense-of-civil-asset-forfeiture-annotated/

Kelly, B. D. (2019). *Fighting crime or raising revenue? Testing opposing views of forfeiture* [Report]. Institute for Justice. https://s3.documentcloud.org/documents/6152037/Fighting-Crime-or-Raising-Revenue.pdf

Knepper, L., McDonald, J., Sanchez, K., & Pohl, E. S. (2020). *Policing for profit: The abuse of civil asset forfeiture* (3rd ed.). Institute for Justice. https://ij.org/wp-content/uploads/2020/12/policing-for-profit-3-web.pdf

Lawyers' Committee for Civil Rights of the San Francisco Bay Area. (2016). *Stopped, fined, arrested: Racial bias in policing and traffic courts in California* [Report]. https://lccrsf.org/wp-content/uploads/Stopped_Fined_Arrested_BOTRCA.pdf

Lawyers' Committee for Civil Rights of the San Francisco Bay Area, East Bay Community Law Center, Western Center on Law & Poverty, A New Way of Life Re-Entry Project, & Legal Services for Prisoners With Children. (2015). *Not just a Ferguson problem: How traffic courts drive inequality in California* [Report]. Western Center on Law & Poverty. https://wclp.org/wp-content/uploads/2015/05/Not-Just-a-Ferguson-Problem-How-Traffic-Courts-Drive-Inequality-in-California.pdf

McDonald, J., & Carpenter, D. M., II. (2021). *Frustrating, corrupt, unfair: Civil forfeiture in the words of its victims* [Report]. Institute for Justice. https://ij.org/report/frustrating-corrupt-unfair/

Office of the Inspector General, U.S. Department of Justice. (2017). *Audit of the Assets Forfeiture Fund and Seized Asset Deposit Fund annual financial statements: Fiscal year 2017* (Report No. 18-05). https://www.oversight.gov/sites/default/files/oig-reports/a1805.pdf

Office of the Inspector General, U.S. Department of Justice. (2021). *Audit of the Assets Forfeiture Fund and Seized Asset Deposit Fund annual financial statements: Fiscal year 2020* (Report No. 21-015). https://oig.justice.gov/sites/default/files/reports/21-015.pdf

Stahl, M. B. (1992). Asset forfeiture, burdens of proof and the war on drugs. *Journal of Criminal Law & Criminology*, *83*(2), 274–337. https://doi.org/10.2307/1143859

Texas Appleseed. (2017). *Defending against a civil asset forfeiture case in Texas: A toolkit for property owners.* http://endforfeitureabusetx.org/sites/default/files/pdfs/caft_finalformattingmarch2017.pdf

U.S. Department of Justice, Asset Forfeiture Program. (2014). *National Asset Forfeiture Strategic Plan 2008–2012.* http://www.justice.gov/criminal/afmls/pubs/pdf/strategicplan.pdf

CHAPTER 03

Drug Caucus in California

Abstract

I n California, possessing a controlled substance, such as illegal drugs like heroin or prescription drugs not obtained with a proper prescription, is against the law. Throughout American history, the justifications proffered in support of anti-narcotics federal law have been said to be grounded in history, scientific research, and public safety. Conversely, proponents of the legalization of drugs have raised fundamental principles of federalism and a lack of effective alternatives to the use of medical marijuana for treating symptoms of many serious illnesses. Several amendments have been made over time since the acquisition, possession, transportation, delivery, production, or use of marijuana under California's medical marijuana laws are still subject to discussion and controversy. In a time when Californians face massive budget cuts and an economic recession due to the COVID-19 pandemic and economic shutdown, it is prudent to revise the drug caucus domestic policy. As of today, the war on narcotics-related policies has been ineffective, inhumane, and expensive. Furthermore, it has even developed the California system of mass incarceration. Thus, we must dismantle and end its vestiges, which are still in place today, according to Governor Gavin Newsom, who signed Senate Bill 73, which became effective on January 1, 2021.

Chapter Summary

California has traditionally been on the cutting edge of marijuana policy reform. Although the war on drugs is not over in the US, California is today probably one of the most liberal and progressive states toward people who consume and inject drugs. However, it was one of the first states to prohibit marijuana in 1913, predating the federal Marihuana Tax Act of 1937 by approximately 25 years. Fighting illicit narcotics has been a shared effort between federal, state, and local agencies, with California accepting a larger percentage of the burden than other states. California adopted mandatory minimum sentences for nonviolent drug crimes during the war on drugs, thus fueling mass incarceration. Since then, experts have widely acknowledged the war on drugs as a racist policy failure—costing vast amounts of money while tearing apart communities and not making us safer. By analyzing the history of drugs in California and its relationship with the dynamic rest of the world, one can provide valuable recommendations to California policymakers.

Introduction to Drug Caucus Policy in California

California's drug wars have shown how state and local governments played relevant roles in the 20th- and 21st-century processes of penalizing drug use, creating drug policy, and enduring enforcement cultures through public policies and procedures. Drug-control policy at every level in the US during the 20th century has prohibited the recreational use of consciousness-altering drugs and, consequently, criminalized and punished users and sellers.

As the study of Amos Irwin et al. (2017) demonstrated, heroin use by young adults has more than doubled in the US in the past two decades, while heroin overdose deaths rose almost 250% from 2010 to 2014, reaching 29 overdoses per day in 2014. Furthermore, the heroin epidemic has also caused enormous infection-related medical costs because many people inject heroin with shared needles in unsterilized environments. Although people who inject drugs comprise less than 1% of the U.S. population, they are thought to experience 56% of new hepatitis C virus (HCV) infections and 11% of new HIV infections. In various emergency rooms, skin and soft tissue infections are the leading cause of hospitalization of people who inject drugs. While the combined medical costs of this relatively tiny population likely exceed $6 billion annually, this information is apparently hidden in individual medical records, masking the need for prevention efforts.

Supervised injection facilities likely provide a safe, controlled, clean place with adequate injection equipment so that people who inject drugs can bring in previously obtained drugs and inject in the presence of medical staff. Approximately 97 supervised injection facilities exist in 66 cities across 11 countries worldwide. The only supervised injection facilities in North America—Insite and the Dr. Peter Centre—are in Vancouver, Canada. Skin and soft tissue health outcomes have been extensively evaluated, demonstrating five principal cost-saving benefits.

First, they reduce HIV and HCV transmission by preventing needle-sharing and providing education. As medical staff provide sterile equipment, advice, and primary wound care, they also reduce the prevalence and seriousness of skin and soft tissue infections, thus preventing clients from dying of an overdose, with no reported overdose deaths in supervised injection facilities worldwide after millions of injections. Furthermore, supervised injection facilities have increased successful uptake into addiction treatment by developing a trusting, positive relationship between health workers and people who inject drugs.

Definitions

California's medical marijuana laws protect those seriously ill and whose health would benefit from using medical marijuana. Nevertheless, California medical marijuana laws do not affect federal laws, and there is no medical exception for the possession or distribution of marijuana under federal law. Definitions related to the California Drug Caucus policy include the following per Medical Marihuana Policy 452–Guidelines for the Security and Non-Diversion of Cannabis Grown for Medical Use (California Department of Justice, Office of the Attorney General, n.d.; University of California Santa Cruz Police Department, n.d.):

- Attending Physician: a person who possesses a license in good standing to practice medicine in California; has taken responsibility for some aspect of the medical care, treatment, diagnosis, counseling, or referral of a patient; and has complied with accepted medical standards in California that a reasonable and prudent physician would follow when recommending or approving medicinal cannabis for the treatment of a patient (Bus. & Prof. Code, § 2525.2, citing §11362.7, subd. [a].)

- Cardholder: someone issued a current identification card

- Compassionate Use Act (CUA; Health and Safety Code § 11362.5): a California law intended to protect from prosecution those who are seriously ill and whose health would likely benefit from the use of marijuana in the treatment of illness for which marijuana provides relief

- Investigation: investigations involving the possession, delivery, production, or use of marijuana usually fall into one of three categories:

    a. investigations when no person makes a medicinal claim,

    b. investigations when a cardholder makes a medicinal claim, and

    c. investigations when a non-cardholder makes a medicinal claim.

  Note: Whenever the preliminary investigation reveals an amount of marijuana more significant than the statutory amount, officers should consider the following factors when determining whether the form and amount are reasonably related to the patient's needs, such as the amount of marijuana recommended by a medical professional to be ingested, the quality of the marijuana, the method of ingestion, the timing of the possession concerning a harvest (patient may be storing marijuana), and if the marijuana was being cultivated indoors or outdoors.

- Medical marijuana: marijuana possessed by a patient or primary caregiver for legitimate medical purposes

- Medical Marijuana Program (MMP; Health and Safety Code § 11362.7 et seq.): California lawmakers passed this program following the Compassionate Use Act to facilitate the prompt identification of patients and their designated primary caregivers to avoid unnecessary arrests and provide needed guidance to law enforcement officers. MMP prohibits arrests for possession of medical marijuana in certain circumstances and provides a defense in others.

- Patient: a person entitled to the protections of the Compassionate Use Act after receiving a recommendation or approval from a physician to use marijuana for medical purposes or any person issued a valid identification card

- Primary caregiver: a person designated by the patient who has consistently assumed responsibility for the patient's housing, health, or safety and who may assist the patient with the medical use of marijuana under the Compassionate Use Act or the MMP (Health and Safety Code § 11362.5; Health and Safety Code § 11362.7)

- Physician's recommendation: Physicians may not prescribe cannabis because the federal Food and Drug Administration regulates prescription drugs and, under the Controlled Substances Act, marijuana is a Schedule I drug, meaning that it has no recognized medical use, with the exception noted above. Nevertheless, physicians may lawfully issue

a written or oral recommendation under California
law indicating that cannabis would be a beneficial
treatment for a serious medical condition.

- Statutory amount: no more than 8 ounces of
  dried, mature, processed female marijuana flowers
  ("bud") or the plant conversion (e.g., kief, hash,
  hash oil), and also no more than six mature or 12
  immature marijuana plants (roots, stems, and stem
  fibers should not be considered; Health and Safety
  Code § 11362.77).

History

According to Dale Gieringer (2006), cannabis was for-
mally introduced to California as hemp by the Spanish,[5]
who farmed it as a fiber crop at the missions. Hemp cul-
ture prospered thanks to Spanish subsidies but collapsed
with their end in 1810 and was brought to California at
Mission San Jose in 1795 with the incentive of Gov. de
Borica. In 1897, the first known reference to Mexican
"mariguana" [not indexed] appeared in the Call. On the
other hand, the Los Angeles Times published four new
articles about marijuana from 1898 to 1911, followed
by more pieces when the Board began its anti-marijuana
campaign in 1914. The term marihuana, in its current
spelling (marijuana), did not appear in Northern Califor-

---

[5] During the early nineteenth century, the Russians also cultivated hemp at
Ft. Ross.

nia until the 1920s. On the other hand, Sacco's (2014) study found the following:

> Both recreational and medical uses of drugs, including cocaine and opium, were popular in the 19th century, but the federal government was not involved in restricting or regulating their distribution and use. During this time, the federal government did not have any agencies that regulated medical and pharmaceutical practice, and doctors freely prescribed cocaine and morphine as a treatment for pain. By the end of the 19th century, abuse of these drugs was a significant social issue, and public concern was growing. Scholars identified the separation of federal and state power as a major reason for an unregulated U.S. drug market in the 19th century. Attempts to establish federal control over drugs were met with strong opposition from patent medicine firms and state officials.

Federal control of drugs began to take shape in the early 20th century. In response to growing levels of drug abuse, the federal government sought to regulate and control drugs through taxation. The Harrison Narcotics Act of 1914 (Harrison Act; P.L. 63–223), among other things, required importers, manufacturers, and distributors of cocaine and opium to register with the U.S. Department of the Treasury (the Treasury), pay a special tax on these drugs, and keep records of each transaction. Under the Harrison Act, practitioners were authorized to prescribe opiates and cocaine; however, the law was subject to interpretation. The Treasury viewed patient drug maintenance using these substances as beyond medical scope, and many physicians were arrested, prosecuted, and jailed. Under the authority of the Harrison Act, the Narcotic Division of the Internal Revenue Bureau closed down state and city narcotic clinics and sent drug violators to federal penitentiaries. Enforcement agents were referred to as "narcs." Ultimately, physicians stopped prescribing drugs covered under the Harrison Act, thereby sending users to the black market to seek out these substances.

During the 1920s, narcotic enforcement was closely tied to Prohibition enforcement. In 1930, Prohibition enforcement was transferred to the Department of Justice, while a standalone federal agency, the Federal Bureau of Narcotics (FBN), was established within the Treasury to handle narcotic enforcement. During Prohibition, a new recreational drug—marijuana—had quickly become unpopular with law enforcement, especially in the southwestern

United States. As Prohibition ended, marijuana caught the attention of Congress and the FBN. Until 1937, the growth and use of marijuana were legal under federal law. During the course of promoting federal legislation to control marijuana, Henry Anslinger, the first commissioner of the FBN, and others submitted testimony to Congress regarding the evils of marijuana use, claiming that it incited violent and insane behavior. Of note, Commissioner Anslinger had informed Congress that "the major criminal in the United States is the drug addict; that of all the offenses committed against the laws of this country, the narcotic addict is the most frequent offender." (pp. 2–3)

Since the last quarter of the 19th century marked the high tide of widespread drug use in the US, numerous anti-narcotics bills were already introduced during the 1880s and 1890, most of which never reached a vote. Although they were mainly aimed at opium, three remarkably included hemp drugs. For many, the epoch is remembered as the dope fiend's paradise. Notably, smoking opium, not cannabis, initially emerged as the drug of interest to pleasure seekers in California. The Chinese introduced opium during the Gold Rush, and the habit initially gave minor offense. On the California Coast, oriental-style hashish houses were thought to be flourishing (Gieringer, 2006).

Eventually, the situation worsened with the economy in the 1870s when anti-Chinese sentiment rose, and the habit spread to Whites. This event forced San Francisco to pass the nation's first anti-narcotic statute. Other American towns and states soon followed suit, including the California legislature, as the nuisance spread across the country with the Chinese. Nevertheless, reiterated legislative efforts failed to eradicate the habit but simply suppressed it from public view, leaving it flourishing in the back alleys of Chinatown and elsewhere for decades to follow.

During the 20th century, the history of California's drug wars showed that state and local governments played leading roles in criminalizing drug use, creating drug policy, and enduring enforcement cultures. Scholars identified the separation of federal and state power as a major reason for an unregulated U.S. drug market in the 19th century. Attempts to establish federal control over drugs were usually met with strong opposition from patent medicine firms and state officials (Sacco, 2014; Siff, 2016).

In response to growing drug abuse and addiction levels, the U.S. federal government sought to regulate and control drugs through taxation. For instance, the Harrison Act of 1914 required importers, manufacturers, and distributors of cocaine and opium to register with the Department of the Treasury, pay a special tax on these narcotics, and keep records of each transaction. Under the Harrison Act, practitioners were authorized to prescribe opiates and cocaine; however, the law was subject to interpretation. Concerning the Marihuana Tax Act of 1937, Lisa Sacco (2014) stated:

> During the 1920s, narcotic enforcement was closely tied to Prohibition enforcement. In 1930, Prohibition enforcement was transferred to the Department of Justice, while a stand-alone federal agency, the Federal Bureau of Narcotics (FBN), was established within the Treasury to handle narcotic enforcement. During Prohibition, a new recreational drug—marijuana—had quickly become unpopular with law enforcement, especially in the southwestern United States. As Prohibition ended, marijuana caught the attention of Congress and the FBN.

> Until 1937, the growth and use of marijuana were legal under federal law. During the course of promoting federal legislation to control marijuana, Henry Anslinger, the first commissioner of the FBN, and others submitted testimony to Congress regarding the evils of marijuana use, claiming that it incited violent and insane behavior. Of note, Commissioner Anslinger had informed Congress that "the major criminal in the United States is the drug addict; that of all the offenses committed

against the laws of this country, the narcotic addict is the most frequent offender."

The federal government unofficially banned marijuana under the Marihuana Tax Act of 1937. The MTA imposed a strict regulation requiring a high-cost transfer tax stamp for every sale of marijuana. These stamps, however, were rarely issued by the federal government. Shortly after the passage of the MTA, all states made the possession of marijuana illegal.

Enforcement of drug laws was primarily the responsibility of local police, and the FBI occasionally assisted with enforcement. Due to limited and reduced appropriations during the Great Depression, which began in the United States after the stock market crash of 1929 and lasted through the 1930s, the FBN budget and the number of narcotic agents declined and remained low for years. Publicity and warnings of the dangers of narcotics, in particular, marijuana, became methods of drug control for the FBN. In seeking federal control of marijuana and uniform narcotic laws, Commissioner Anslinger made personal appeals to civic groups and legislators and pushed for, and received, editorial support in newspapers; many newspapers maintained a steady stream

of anti-marijuana propaganda in the 1930s.
(pp. 3–4)

Over the following decades, the U.S. Congress continued to pass drug-control legislation and further criminal-
ize drug abuse. The Boggs Act, passed in 1951, established
mandatory prison sentences for some drug offenses, while
the 1956 Narcotic Control Act further increased penalties for drug offenses and established the death penalty as
punishment for selling heroin to youth.

Siff (2016) suggested that the state-level cultural and
political history of the U.S. is fundamental to understanding the drug wars. In this sense, California developed anti-
drug statutes and narcotics enforcement agencies long
before they became trappings of the federal drug wars,
and police in the state enjoyed wide discretion in developing methods to enforce state drug laws from the early
1900s. Political disputes over drug policy were far hotter
and richer at the state level, especially around the mid-
20th century.

Amid the growing paranoia of the Cold War years
and as the greater Los Angeles area flourished in the
years after World War II, drugs were considered a
mysterious, exotic, and calculated foreign threat. While
the threat's place of origin was open for public debate,
the three common suspects were the mafia, communist
China, and Mexico. Settling down to a middle-class
lifestyle in the Los Angeles suburbs, Californians grew

increasingly concerned about drug use among children and teenagers, partly because of their outsized population and urban conditions. While Californians wanted to solve this increasingly dangerous problem with cross-border controls and coercive drug diplomacy in Mexico, federal officials were finding an argument against communist Asia. As early as 1924, reformer Richmond P. Hobson claimed that a conspiratorial three-pronged attack on the US was underway in the form of opium from Asia, cocaine from South America, and "heroin and synthetic drugs" from Europe. Other relevant figures pointed to Britain, Turkey, Greece, Germany, and Japan attempting to fatally undermine the American project with addictive drugs (pp. 22–24, 28).

The abovementioned situation demonstrates that, at least in part, the stigma associated with drug consumption has been historically correlated with public policy objectives, especially foreign ones. It has served to "prove" that international rivals were doing their best to weaken the American nation from the inside. However, as real evidence mounted that more heroin and marijuana in the greater Los Angeles area (California) came from Mexico than from China, Californians grew more alarmed and accusatory toward their neighbor. Then, narcotics became not only associated with communism and anti-Americanism but also with poverty, prostitution, gambling, abortion, mafia, and organized crime.

The FBN continued to enforce federal narcotic laws and support local enforcement, while the agency remained relatively unchanged until the 1960s.[6] Support for severe punishment for drug offenses waned by this point. Organizations, including the American Bar Association, started to speak out against strict punishments for drug offenders while federal support for a medical approach to drug abuse increased. For illustration, methadone maintenance became an acceptable and common treatment for heroin dependence. In 1963, the Presidential Commission On Narcotic and Drug Abuse (the 1963 Presidential Commission) issued a report recommending more funds for narcotic research, less strict punishment for drug offenses, and the dismantling of the FBN (Sacco, 2014).

During the 1960s, the U.S. Congress also began to support the medical approach to addressing drug abuse. The institution heeded the recommendations of the 1963 Commission and created the Bureau of Drug Abuse Control within the Department of Health, Education, and Welfare, and provided for the civil commitment of some drug-addicted federal detainees.

Later, President Nixon's war on drugs involved greater emphasis on law enforcement during the 1970s. He also enhanced international efforts and successfully pushed to curb opium production in Turkey. Nixon pushed for the passage of comprehensive federal drug laws to enhance

---

[6] The agency was dissolved in 1968.

federal control of drugs and narcotics. For instance, the Controlled Substances Act placed the control of select plants, drugs, and chemical substances under federal jurisdiction. Congress passed this legislation, which replaced previous federal drug laws with a single comprehensive statute.

In July 1973, President Nixon authorized the creation of a single-mission federal agency to enforce the Controlled Substances Act: the DEA, which is still operating and is known for being very active, especially in the Americas. Both the committee and President Nixon highlighted the importance of the DEA's role in ensuring cooperation and coordination among the DEA, Federal Bureau of Investigation (FBI), and other DOJ agencies involved and engaged in counterdrug operations. Siff (2016) explained,

> As the Cold War progressed, U.S. narcotic foreign policy became more obviously subordinate to national security objectives; that is, the United States began to prosecute the international drug war in a highly selective fashion. Anslinger's desire to grow his agency, increase his power base, and maintain his own relevance in the face of shifting postwar concerns greatly exacerbated this trend. And he was a hardline, moralistic anticommunist. As a key member of the China lobby, Anslinger worked to help legitimize Nationalist China in spite

of its widespread trade in and consumption of opium. This entailed ignoring evidence submitted by his own agents that communist China's narcotics trade was a small fraction of that feeding Chaing Kai-shek's regime, while forcefully promoting in the American press the belief that most of the heroin that reached U.S. shores came from "Red China" as a plot to undermine its citizens' ability to function. (p. 8)

It stands to reason that Anslinger[7] would have been less able to control the nature of the U.S. relationship with Mexico after World War II than he could with China because the State Department actively pursued good relations with Mexico. Diplomatic considerations were far more important, and Mexico was understandably off-put by U.S. forays into their territory regardless of what was smuggled across the border. The extent of cultivation and use of the drugs in Mexico was never perfectly clear. Anslinger's testimony on Mexico as a source of smuggled drugs and on the anti-drug activities of Mexican officials varied from year to year and was often qualitative. (pp. 29–30)

[7] Harry J. Anslinger was the most influential figure in the drug wars from his appointment as the first commissioner of the Federal Bureau of Narcotics (FBN) in 1930 until his retirement in 1962. He later represented the United States on the United Nations Commission on Narcotic Drugs (CND).

Heroin abuse was the primary concern of the U.S. government in the 1960s and 1970s, so the rising popularity of cocaine and a new form of cocaine referred to as crack led to a renewed demand from the American public that something needed to be done about drug abuse. By 1989, 27% of the American public perceived that drugs, or drug abuse, was the country's most crucial problem as compared to four years prior, in 1985, when only 2% gave this response. Just as Nixon did, President Reagan stressed the importance of criminal justice agencies in the federal government's efforts to combat drug abuse. As the number of federal drug convictions rose sharply between 1980 and 1986, many experts consider that the 1980s were a decade of rising anti-narcotics enforcement. The number of individuals convicted of federal drug offenses more than doubled from 5,244 in 1980 to 12,285 in 1986. These statistics accounted for 51% of the total number of persons convicted of all federal offenses, which increased from 29,952 in 1980 to 43,802 in 1986. The Comprehensive Crime Control Act of 1984 and the Anti-Drug Abuse Acts of 1986 and 1988 were passed during this period (Sacco, 2014).

Since the 1990s, most federal drug legislation over the last 30 years has addressed concerns over synthetic drugs. In the 1990s, the Clinton Administration developed and implemented strategies and policy initiatives to reduce methamphetamine trafficking, production, and abuse. The DEA dedicated over 200 positions to this purpose, and agencies involved in the High-Intensity Drug Trafficking Areas Program targeted methamphetamine operations in the Southwest, where methamphetamine first gained relevance in the US. The DEA assisted state and local law enforcement with methamphetamine lab cleanups and training.

The laws ruling the usage, production, and distribution of marijuana in California have been in flux for the past 30 years. In 1996, voters passed Proposition 215, allowing medical patients to possess and cultivate marijuana to treat their conditions. Proposition 215 was written to allow for a broad interpretation of the conditions under which production and distribution were permitted. In 2003, the California legislature tried to clarify matters by passing a law known as Chapter 875, allowing any Californian with a physician's written permission to own as many as six marijuana plants or possess up to half a pound of marijuana (Kilmer et al., 2010).

Background

The U.S. drug crisis is rapidly growing, and California leads the nation in drug use and consumption. Until recently, Fresno County has been leading in methamphetamine production in California. This drug crisis has a destructive effect, causing loss of income, mental diseases, dysfunctional families, poverty, child abuse, increased crime rates, and death (Cunniff et al., 2008). For instance, former Republican California Governor Schwarzenegger supported various preventative initiatives and eradicating measures; however, the methamphetamine problem has been well-rooted and keeps arising in unsuspecting areas using varied and creative methods.

Kilmer et al. (2010) highlighted that rates of marijuana use in California are reasonably similar to those of the rest of the country. The percentage of Californians 12 and over reporting marijuana use in the previous 30 days was 7% in 2007, compared to 6% for the rest of the nation. For the youngest category, ages 12–17, the difference between California and the rest of the nation was even more negligible. There were also strong similarities in the rates for alcohol and cocaine use, but not for past-month tobacco use, for which the rate is 29% nationally but only 23% for California.

A recent phenomenon in the US and other Western countries is a substantial increase in individuals seeking treatment for marijuana abuse or dependence. Nationally, marijuana now accounts for the most significant number of treatment episodes (excluding alcohol)—approximately 322,000 in 2008, compared to 92,500 in 1992–1993. In that period, the share of treatment admissions for marijuana as the primary drug grew from approximately 6% to 17% (p. 7).

California has seen an even more considerable increase, with a near quintupling of marijuana admissions between 1992 and 2008 (7,300 to almost 35,000, respectively), while the total number of treatment admissions for illicit drugs increased 50% during that period. One understanding of the rise in treatment admissions is that it shows increasing enforcement of marijuana laws. Thus, people seek treatment less to deal with a substance-abuse issue than to manage a legal problem. Nevertheless, other countries, including the Netherlands, where users are not subject to criminal justice pressure as in the US, have seen a similar increase, indicating other factors might be driving or influencing this phenomenon.

U.S.-Mexico violence statistics are impressive. In 2007, approximately 2,500 Mexicans lost their lives in drug trafficking organizations that induced violence. As of July 2008, the death toll was 2,000, exceeding 4,000 by the end of the year. Deaths associated with drug cartels in Mexico in less than two years exceeded the number of coalition troops killed in Iraq since 2003. The homicide rate in Tijuana in the first half of 2008 was 11 times that of Los Angeles during the same time. The United Nations estimates that the illicit narcotics business in Mexico is worth at least $142 billion, approximately 11% of Mexico's gross domestic product (Longmire & Longmire, 2008).

While Californians have debated legalization for decades, the idea is now being taken more seriously by policymakers, pundits, and the general population. It was remarkable when republican Governor Arnold Schwarzenegger suggested that "it was time for a debate" about marijuana legalization to increase state revenues. Moreover, in their study, Kilmer et al. (2010) explained the following:

Decisionmakers should view skeptically any projections that claim either precision or accuracy. In particular, we highlight two distinct drivers of uncertainty that surround these estimates of consumption and tax revenues: uncertainty about parameters (such as how legalization will affect production costs and price) and uncertainty about structural assumptions (such as the federal response to a state that allows production and distribution of a substance that would still be illegal under federal law). Such uncertainties are so large that altering just a few key assumptions or parameter values can dramatically change the results.

With that crucial caveat in mind, we offer the following key insights derived from developing and using this model:

- The pretax retail price of marijuana will substantially decline, likely by more than 80 percent. The price that consumers face will depend heavily on taxes, the structure of the regulatory regime, and how taxes and regulations are enforced.

- Consumption will increase, but it is unclear how much because we know neither the shape of the demand curve nor the level of tax evasion (which reduces revenues and the prices that consumers face).

- Tax revenues could be dramatically lower or higher than the $1.4 billion estimate; for example, there is uncertainty about potential tax revenues that California might derive from taxing marijuana used by residents of other states (e.g., from "drug tourism").

- Previous studies find that the annual costs of enforcing marijuana laws range from around $200 million to nearly $1.9 billion; our estimates show that the costs are probably less than $300 million.

- There is considerable uncertainty about the impact of legalizing marijuana in California on public budgets and consumption, with even minor changes in assumptions leading to major differences in outcomes.

- Much of the research used to inform this debate is based on insights from studies that examine small changes in either marijuana prices or the risk of being sanctioned for possession. The proposed legislation in California would create a

> large change in policy. As a result, it is
> uncertain how useful these studies are
> for making projections about marijuana
> legalization. (p. 2)

Furthermore, marijuana offenses account for most of the narcotic arrests in the US, and the number has increased sharply in the last 30 years. Thus, more than 80% of marijuana arrests are for simple possession. The rate of U.S. possession arrests per capita grew sharply in the 1990s, from approximately 89 per 100,000 in 1991 to 223 in 1997. However, since then, the number has risen more steadily, approaching 250 per 100,000 in 2008 (approximately 750,000 arrests in total). Sales arrests rose even more slowly from 1990 to 2008; instead of the nearly 200% increase for possession, sales arrests nationally rose only about 40% between 1990 and 2008. While per capita marijuana arrests were similar for the US and California in the early 1990s, the subsequent increase was more pronounced outside California.

Still, the arrest data for California also showed a dramatic increase from 1990 to 1996. Per capita, marijuana arrests in California remained stable between 1996 and 2005 (approximately 175 per 100,000), jumping more than 25% between 2005 and 2008. There was a significant increase in total juvenile marijuana arrests in California in the early 1990s, but that number shortly stabilized and has hovered at about 15,000 annually since 1995 (p. 7).

San Diego-Mexico Border Controls

Violence along the U.S.-Mexico border, especially near the San Diego-Tijuana area, has been the focus of political controversy for years since there are many concerning issues involved in this situation: the flow of billions of dollars worth of illicit drug trafficking, the illegal movement into Mexico of assault weapons purchased in U.S. border states, human smuggling rings and trafficking mafias bringing special interest aliens into the US, the potential for terrorists and criminals to enter the US via the southwest border, and ultimately, the induced violence that has spilled over into U.S. border communities.

According to Timothy Dunn (2001), the U.S. military's drug enforcement role engaged in ongoing domestic law enforcement for the first time in over a century during the 1990s. The military provided a vast array of support for civilian police. Its role ranged from providing military equipment and construction work to military training and transport and using ground troops to assist the police. Congress even seriously considered more extreme measures, such as military patrols of urban areas. Much of this military support has focused on the U.S.-Mexico border region. Notably, the border effort is part of the military nationwide domestic anti-drug activity, which receives most of its anti-drug funding.

On the violent and dysfunctional atmosphere that surrounds the drug trade cartels that operate near the border, Pansters and Smith's (2021) research found the following:

Commentators claim that there always has been an inextricable link between the Sinaloa drug trade and violence. For the snooty elites of the state capital, it was a matter of class. Highland rancheros were short on refinement, quick to temper, and proficient with a gun. According to the mayor of Culiacán, the criminals had "come down from the sierra," were "particularly ignorant and spendthrift" and were "easily recognizable by their peculiar form of clothes and walk." For security experts, it is the organization of the trade. The former head of the Mexican security services, Guillermo Valdés Castellanos, argued that violence is always in the DNA of the narcotic business.

Yet, gazing back over the three decades leading up to the outbreak of violence in the mid-1970s, two things become clear. First, Sinaloa and the state capital had been at the heart of the Mexican drug trade since at least the early 1940s. Federal Bureau of Narcotics reports, Congressional investigations, PJF annual reports, the confessions of border drug smugglers, and countless news articles all emphasized the state's predominance in the growing of opium poppies and, at least since around 1947, the production of morphine and heroin. Second, from the early 1940s to the 1970s, violence in the state was relatively low. During the 1950s, criminologist Alfonso Quiroz Cuarón tried to discover the true figures for homicides by avoiding official statistics and tabulating those mentioned in the Civil Registry. He found that the average for Mexico as a whole was 38.2 per 100,000. But, there was enormous regional variation. Ten states had murder rates over 50 per 100,000. In comparison, Sinaloa was only the sixteenth most violent, with a rate of 33.7 per 100,000, just above Querétaro and considerably less than the national average.

Even if it is debatable that consuming marijuana induces violent behavior, American public opinion associated its consumption with the lower social classes of Mexico since they were thought to be their main customers. As Dale Gieringer (2006) stressed, the U.S. Department of Agriculture Bureau of Plant Industry even once announced it had succeeded in growing domestic cannabis of equal quality to the Indians. It is worth considering that up to World War I, pharmaceutical supplies of *cannabis indica* were almost entirely imported from India, per the United States Pharmacopeia, which specified that it came from flowering tops of the Indian variety.

Apart from the historical association of Mexican drug cartels with poverty and violence, some researchers have argued that they work and function as terrorist organizations. According to Longmire and Longmire (2008), who both worked for the U.S. Air Force, the tactics, strategy, organization, and even (at least to a limited extent) the goals of the Mexican drug cartels are consistent with those of recognized terrorist organizations. Moreover, as cocaine's popularity waned and methamphetamine abuse rose, most of the more extensive clandestine labs that produced methamphetamine were in California and Mexico. The DEA did as much as possible to dismantle its networks (Sacco, 2014). Consequently, one can understand the importance of areas like the San Diego-Mexico border because of the high drug trafficking networks operating there.

Policymaking in California

Understanding that a public policy is a government plan of action to solve the problems people share collectively or cannot solve on their own, one can think of policies as courses of action by creating operational principles to accomplish desired goals. Drug enforcement-related policies are part of the state domestic policies, which create standard operational procedures by which a government operates.

In 1996, California became the first state to officially allow medicinal cannabis use when voters passed the Compassionate Use Act in 1996. Today, cannabis is legal in California for medicinal and adult recreational use under certain conditions. The cannabis industry is strictly regulated in California to ensure the drug is kept away from children, businesses can operate safely, and products are contaminant-free and properly labeled to inform purchasers. According to the California Department of Justice, Office of the Attorney General's (n.d.) Guidelines for the Security and Non-Diversion of Cannabis Grown for Medical Use,

> On November 5, 1996, California voters passed Proposition 215, the Compassionate Use Act (CUA), which decriminalized the cultivation, possession, and use of marijuana by seriously ill individuals upon a physician's recommendation (§ 11362.5.). The CUA was enacted to "ensure that seriously ill Californians have the right to obtain and use marijuana for medical purposes where that medical use is deemed appropriate and has been recommended by a physician who has determined that the person's health would benefit from the use of marijuana," "ensure that patients and their primary caregivers who obtain and use marijuana for medical purposes upon the recommendation of a physician are not subject to criminal prosecution or sanction," and "encourage federal and state governments to implement a plan for the safe and affordable distribution of marijuana to all

patients in medical need of marijuana" The CUA is a narrowly drafted statute designed to allow a qualified medical patient and his or her primary caregiver to possess and cultivate marijuana for the patient's personal use.

The CUA states that "Section 11357, relating to the possession of marijuana, and Section11358, relating to the cultivation of marijuana, shall not apply to a patient, or to a patient's primary caregiver, who possesses or cultivates marijuana for the personal medical purposes of the patient upon the written or oral recommendation or approval of a physician" Accordingly, the CUA is designed to ensure that Californians who comply with the CUA are not subject to criminal sanctions.

Since its enactment, uncertainties in the act have become apodictic, impeding law enforcement's ability to interpret and suitably execute the law. Police challenges with enforcing the act have encountered difficulties distinguishing between legitimate and illegitimate marijuana usage. Federal and California state courts have filtered through often shady issues in adjudicating charges against defendants claiming protection under the act. For instance, various California counties, taking matters into their own hands, have developed and adopted programs to implement the 1996 Compassionate Use Act, thus contributing further to the disparity in the statewide application.

The Compassionate Use Act only provides limited immunity as a defense in court. Police officers can still arrest anyone who grows too much marijuana or tries to sell it. Consequently, the provisions and protections under the act are limited, and the acts of selling, giving away, transporting, and growing large quantities of marijuana remained criminal (McCabe, 2004).

On January 1, 2004, Senate Bill 420, the Medical Marijuana Program Act, a separate legislative scheme implementing the Compassionate Use Act, became law. This act required the California Department of Public Health to develop and maintain a program for the voluntary enrollment of qualified medicinal cannabis patients and their primary caregivers via a statewide identification card system. Based on a physician's recommendation, medical cannabis identification cards were thought to help law enforcement officers identify and verify that cardholders can cultivate, deliver, transport, and possess specific amounts of medicinal cannabis. Under specific conditions, they would not be subject to fines or arrest (California Department of Justice, Office of the Attorney General, n.d.).

County health departments must verify the applicant's status as a qualified patient before issuing the identification card. State and local law enforcement have immediate access to information to verify the card's validity. The Medical Marijuana Program Act also defined certain terms and set possession guidelines for cardholders.

On October 11, 2015, Senate Bill 643, Assembly Bill 266, and Assembly Bill 243, collectively known as the Medical Marijuana Regulation and Safety Act, were signed into law. This act established a state regulatory and licensing system for the cultivation, manufacturing, delivery, and sale of medicinal cannabis as of January 1, 2016. Since 2016, recreational marijuana has been legal in California. Several new cannabis laws are now in effect in California for 2022.

On November 8, 2016, the California voters passed Proposition 64, better known as the Control, Regulate, and Tax Adult-Use of Marijuana Act, creating a comprehensive system to legalize, control, and properly regulate the cultivation, processing, manufacture, distribution, sale, and testing of non-medical marijuana, including marijuana products, for use by adults 21 years and older while providing for the taxation of the commercial growth and retail sale of marijuana. In 2017, the MMRSA was repealed by Senate Bill 94, the Medicinal and Adult-Use Cannabis Regulation and Safety Act. The intent was to combat the illegal market by creating a regulatory and formal structure to govern California commercial cannabis activity, preventing minors' access and protecting public safety, public health, and the overall environment (p. 3).

On June 27, 2017, Senate Bill 94, the Medicinal and Adult-Use Cannabis Regulation and Safety Act (MAU-CRSA), was passed into law. This act reduced and eliminated certain criminal penalties related to cannabis and continued to exempt qualified patients and their primary caregivers from certain criminal penalties. However, most criminal offenses related to cannabis for a person 18 years or older are punishable as an infraction or misdemeanor.

Still today, arrests are one of the public policies associated with marijuana possession and distribution. It is crucial to have data on these arrests' dispositions to assess the personal consequences and estimate the current costs of marijuana enforcement. Since state law indicates that those possessing less than one ounce are generally supposed to be cited without booking, we can safely infer that most of the subjects arrested for simple possession are not incarcerated. California law has determined a fine as the maximum penalty for decades now. Indeed, when Proposition 36 gave those arrested for simple possession of any drug for the first or second time a treatment alternative to criminal justice sanctioning, most marijuana arrestees chose not to engage in this diversion program because they already faced so little threat of jail (Kilmer et al., 2010).

Policymakers must manage the situation carefully per other issues California is facing, such as mass incarceration. The legalization of drugs may alleviate social issues and even help with the California budget process since they use those funds in other strategic areas.

Recommendations

High-quality scientific evidence suggests that supervised drug consumption effectively facilitates the achievement of California public health and order objectives with a lack of adverse impacts and, therefore, supports their role as part of a continuum of services to support Californians and improve the quality of life of the state residents. Since these facilities remain under-utilized in many places globally, policymakers require more evidence to better understand how to address the problem and further adjust their policy agendas.

Supervised injection facilities have notably reduced health care, emergency services, and crime costs. Establishing an in-site supervised injection facility would save roughly $6.1 million per year. This policy would be cost-effective as the facility would cost roughly $2.6 million annually, and experts have estimated that every dollar spent would generate $2.33 in savings. A single facility would greatly impact citywide, given the significant net savings of $3.5 million. Enforcing marijuana laws imposes costs on criminal justice agencies (Irwin et al., 2017; Kilmer et al., 2010). Since the costs associated with the laws implemented due to the war on drugs are high, and the results have been quite poor thus far, it seems convenient to keep developing another strategy, as the California government has recently been doing.

Considering that people who use drugs may give socially desirable responses during research interviews, it is essential to address the potential limitations that studies on supervised drug consumption facilities can have, as highlighted by McNeil et al. (2014). By providing assistance injecting in a regulated environment and under a harm reduction policy, supervised drug consumption facilities can mitigate barriers and, in turn, function to establish safer injecting habits and supply an escape from day-to-day violence. Furthermore, California drug user-led organizations can play a central role in developing harm reduction programs and may be highly proactive and responsive to emerging trends within the drug user community.

To protect the rights of every California resident, policymakers and lawmakers should avoid creating loopholes in the best interest. New legislation must be clear and understandable since the opposite may open the door to potential abuses by recommending physicians and persons wishing to gain access to marijuana, for example. Drug trends will likely evolve along with law enforcement responses to drug crimes, but the same fundamental issues will probably continue to confront lawmakers. The road to full yet safe legalization may be the best long-term scenario.

References

California Department of Justice, Office of the Attorney General. (n.d.). *Guidelines for the security and non-diversion of cannabis grown for medical use*. Retrieved August 10, 2022, from http://oag.ca.gov/system/files/attachments/press-docs/MEDICI-NAL%20CANNABIS%20Guidelines.pdf

Cunniff, J., Cunniff, D. T., & Kay, K. D. (2008). The crisis of meth-amphetamine and its management: Preparation, participation, and prevention. *Contemporary Issues in Education Research*, *1*(2), 1–8. http://files.eric.ed.gov/fulltext/EJ1056473.pdf

Dunn, T. J. (2001). Border militarization via drug and immigration enforcement: Human rights implications. *Social Justice*, *28*(2), 7–30. https://www.jstor.org/stable/29768073

Gieringer, D. H. (2006). *The origins of cannabis prohibition in California*. Federal Legal Publications. www.canorml.org/wp-content/uploads/2019/04/caloriginsmjproh.pdf

Irwin, A., Jozaghi, E., Bluthenthal, R. N., & Kral, A. H. (2017). A cost-benefit analysis of a potential supervised injection facility in San Francisco, California, USA. *Journal of Drug Issues*, *47*(2), 164–184. https://doi.org/10.1177/0022042616679829

Kilmer, B., Caulkins, J. P., Pacula, R. L., MacCoun, R. J., & Reuter, P. H. (2010). *Altered state?: Assessing how marijuana legalization in California could influence marijuana consumption and public budgets* [Occasional paper]. RAND Corporation. https://www. rand.org/content/dam/rand/pubs/occasional_papers/2010/ RAND_OP315.pdf

Longmire, S. M., & Longmire, J. P. (2008). Redefining terrorism: Why Mexican drug trafficking is more than just organized crime. *Journal of Strategic Security*, *1*(1), 35–52. https://doi. org/10.5038/1944-0472.1.1.4

McCabe, T. L. (2004). Health and safety / It's high time: California attempts to clear the smoke surrounding the Compassionate Use Act. *McGeorge Law Review*, *35*(3), Article 21. https:// scholarlycommons.pacific.edu/mlr/vol35/iss3/21

McNeil, R., Small, W., Lampkin, H., Shannon, K., & Kerr, T. (2014). "People knew they could come here to get help": An ethnographic study of assisted injection practices at a peer-run 'unsanctioned' supervised drug consumption room in a Canadian setting. *AIDS and Behavior*, *18*(3), 473–485. https://doi. org/10.1007/s10461-013-0540-y

Pansters, W. G., & Smith, B. T. (2021). *La mafia muere*: Violence, drug trade and the state in Sinaloa, 1940-1980. *European Review of Latin American and Caribbean Studies*, (112), 91–116. https:// www.jstor.org/stable/48658261

Sacco, L. N. (2014). *Drug enforcement in the United States: History, policy, and trends* [Report]. Congressional Research Service. http://sgp.fas.org/crs/misc/R43749.pdf

Siff, S. B. (2016). *Tough on dope: Crime and politics in California's drug wars, 1946-1963* [Doctoral dissertation, The Ohio State University].

University of California Santa Cruz Police Department. (2020). Policy 452: Medical marijuana. In *UC Santa Cruz PD policy manual*, from https://police.ucsc.edu/report/policies/chapter-400/ medical_marijuana.pdf

Social Costs of Invisible Walls in California: Housing Insecurity and Residential Segregation

Social Costs of Invisible Walls in California: Housing Insecurity and Residential Segregation

I t is no secret that, excluding Hawaii, California has the highest average property prices and rentals in the United States (World Population Review, n.d.). There is a vast body of literature on how unwarranted restrictions on housing supply and poor, shortsighted urban planning are driving up California's housing costs (Johnson et al., 2020; Woetzel et al., 2016). Since housing is the most essential human need, it goes without saying that high housing costs constitute a political concern.

Without ensuring housing, it is evident that people will be unable to meet any other human needs, deprived of many areas of human growth. Higher housing expenses reduce spending on many other necessities and priorities, including food, education, health care, entertainment, and the arts. The future aspirations of individuals and families that spend a significant portion of their income on housing are severely diminished. Individuals who spend a substantial income on rent cannot contribute to themselves or society. A depressive gloom can envelop the individual and their family.

Housing insecurity is frequently considered in conjunction with high housing costs. Housing insecurity is not merely a concern for individuals or families since your neighborhood and rental rate can have long-lasting consequences on future generations. Your neighborhood can tremendously affect you and your children's vocational and academic education, the chance of committing crimes, and the likelihood of finding more lucrative or gratifying employment. Therefore, housing insecurity is not merely a measure of economic disparity. It is a matter of policy with far-reaching and far-reaching societal ramifications (Leopold et al., 2022).

However, housing insecurity is not the only issue due to California's high housing costs. The negative social consequences of housing insecurity should be considered in conjunction with residential segregation. Due to housing insecurity, California's underserved population is relegated to residing in severely segregated neighborhoods. Although residential segregation cannot be reduced by housing costs alone, de facto segregation rooted in housing insecurity imposes substantial societal costs (Cohen & Wardrip, 2011).

This piece does not provide policy recommendations on California's excessive housing costs and rental rates. In another book, I have elaborated on how California's housing regulations, which have been in place for decades, artificially inflate property prices, and what policies can be implemented to address this serious social problem. Here, I discuss the California housing crisis in the context of housing insecurity and residential segregation, including the profound social disparities and far-reaching social problems resulting from this crisis. In this context, it is essential to define the idea of housing insecurity before identifying the issue.

How Big Is California's Housing Insecurity Problem?

Housing insecurity is characterized by high housing costs relative to people's wages, poor housing conditions, and unstable neighborhoods (Leopold et al., 2022). According to experts, the likelihood of housing instability increases when individuals allocate more than 30% of their income to housing costs (Pew Charitable Trusts, 2016), which could be because property prices are rapidly increasing, earnings are decreasing, and the economy is not as productive as it was. All these factors contribute to housing insecurity.

California's economy is one of the largest and most productive in the US and the world. The situation of housing insecurity in California cannot be attributed to economic growth or productivity. There are considerably more specific causes that can be resolved much more quickly than an economic crisis. The most significant factor contributing to housing insecurity in California is the consistent and persistent rise in home prices. However, many low-income individuals and families in California endure housing instability due to a decline in income, particularly under the COVID-19 pandemic.

Housing insecurity can be experienced in various forms by different individuals and families. Individuals may share their houses with a larger-than-average number of people, they may have to frequently move because they cannot afford the rent, and they may have trouble affording utilities such as heating, electricity, and gas. Individuals and families may confront even more difficult living circumstances. The most severe type of housing insecurity is homelessness, which includes residing in a shelter, a vehicle, or a tent in a public location (Family Promise of Southern Ocean County, 2021).

It might be difficult for upper-income groups to identify with housing insecurities unless they are homeless due to the different housing insecurity types. However, widespread housing insecurity exists, while the average American associates homelessness with mental illness or substance abuse. These factors are undeniably significant contributors to the issue of homelessness. However, in places where the number of homeless people is higher than the national average, especially in California, high property prices and rents relative to income are the primary cause of homelessness. For this reason, homelessness rates above the national average significantly signal housing insecurity.

The problem of housing insecurity, which is easily solvable with accurate and consistent policies, leads to numerous significant societal problems that cannot be quickly resolved, perpetuating intergenerational disparity. Those who experience housing insecurity are more likely to lose their jobs and be incarcerated, leading to a lower chance of finding employment in a satisfying job. Moreover, people residing in overcrowded houses are more prone to physical and mental health issues. There is a statistically significant decline in the academic career and the prospects of students who regularly move. In neighborhoods that are becoming more impoverished, the incentives for criminal activity increase (Healthy People, n.d.).

Importantly, the implications of all these challenges are not restricted to individual lives; rather, they drive future generations to fight for their lives under more challenging conditions. This vicious cycle also increases social and economic inequality between generations. Therefore, living in a safe neighborhood with decent schools and proximity to one's place of employment is also crucial for economic success. However, a shortage of affordable housing can confine low-income families to unstable neighborhoods with substandard schools and few employment opportunities.

Unquestionably, excessive housing costs are not the only cause of the aforementioned societal issues. However, the overall state affects the socioeconomic conditions of the neighborhood and the lives of individuals and families. According to research, moving from a low-income to an average-income neighborhood significantly improves families' living conditions and future chances, particularly for students (Chetty et al., 2016). Consequently, where we reside can have profound effects on our life. The extensive effects of our neighborhood's environment on our lives give housing insecurity significance.

These disturbing socioeconomic issues in California are accelerating ghettoization, heightening de facto segregation, and posing a serious threat to the social fabric. In numerous ways, the aforementioned issues are connected to high housing costs. For this reason, I begin the debate with statistical data revealing the scope of California housing insecurity.

Figure 1

California housing insecurity scope

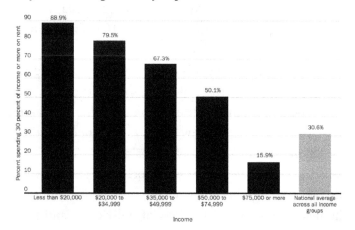

American Communities Survey, U.S. Census Bureau, 2018

The smaller your income is, the greater your expenditures. Although economists suggest we should not spend more than 30% of our income on housing, one-third of income-earning Americans spend 40%. The average percentage of income spent on housing across all income categories in the US is 30.6%. It is common knowledge that California's predicament is worse than the national average since 80% or more of Californians with low incomes experience home insecurity. Although it is obvious that there is a housing problem for low-income families, it is vital to examine the figures to see that housing insecurity also affects middle-income families since 37% of families with a middle income spend more than 30% of their income on housing (Tanner, 2021).

By comparing California house prices and rentals to the national average, we can better comprehend how housing costs contribute to poverty in California. The Federal Reserve Bank of St. Louis reported that the average U.S. home price in 2021 was $374,900. The Zillow Home Value Index estimated that the average house price in 2021 was $293,349. In comparison, the Federal Reserve Bank of St. Louis estimated that the average home price in California in 2021 was $683,996. According to a study by The Hoover Institute, fewer than one-third of Californian families can afford the median housing price. Additionally, this figure includes homes with multiple earners. In places like San Francisco and Santa Clara County, this rate falls to 15% (Fernández-Villaverde & Ohanian, 2018).

When California rentals are compared to the national average, the housing insecurity of individuals who cannot afford a home becomes more apparent. The average rent for a two-bedroom apartment in California is $1,500 a month.

The national median rent is $1,098 per month. If you think these rentals are expensive, you may be shocked by the typical rents in Los Angeles or San Francisco. Renting a home in these cities cost more than $3,000 a month. In addition, housing costs and rents continue to climb rapidly. Six of the 15 most expensive housing rental markets in the US are in California. Consequently, two-thirds of low-income Californians are concerned that their family members may be unable to pay rent in the future (U.S. Census Bureau, 2018, 2021).

Figure 2

National cost of two-bedroom apartment

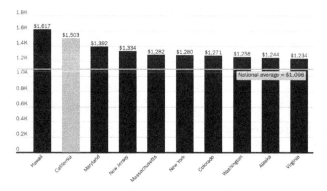

Source: Average Rent by State 2021, World Population Review

The Census Bureau reports that 12.5% of Californians are poor. However, when the Supplemental Poverty Measure (SPM) is considered, 18.1% of Californians are poor. SPM is an index that considers crucial factors not included in official poverty measurements (U.S. Census Bureau, 2021). Housing costs are the most important component of the SPM. California has the greatest level of housing-cost-related poverty in the US.

According to data from the National Low-Income Housing Coalition, there is a shortage of 1,003,595 affordable rental houses for extremely low-income tenants. Californians live in houses twice as crowded as the national average, according to 2018 data (National Low Income Housing Coalition, n.d.). After Utah, California has the second-fewest residents per capita. This figure is 15% lower than the national average. When future aspirations are considered, it is anticipated that California has a shortage of 3.5 million housing units. Therefore, almost 200,000 new homes must be constructed annually to meet the current demand for housing in California (Woetzel et al., 2016).

Figure 3

Household types living in crowded housing

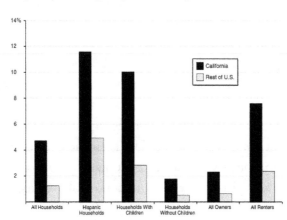

Source: Legislative Analyst Office, 2015

Housing Costs and Residential Segregation in California

As previously discussed, housing insecurity is prevalent in California. However, residential segregation considerably raises its societal cost. According to researchers, the growth of residential segregation is explained by socio-economic inequality, group prejudice, and housing discrimination (Williams & Collins, 2001). Explanations of segregation based on socioeconomic status primarily refer to income disparities. Differences in money and status frequently cause residential segregation, as Hispanics, African Americans, and other minorities work in lower-status and lower-paying occupations and receive a substandard education.

Intuitively, income disparities are considered the leading source of residential segregation. However, evidence indicates that they are less influential than other factors in de facto segregation. For instance, research for Los Angeles County revealed that ethnic and racial characteristics mostly determine ethnoracial residential segregation (Paul et al., 2016). In this setting, racial preferences and institutional racism have a greater impact than income disparities and social status. Similarly, African American homeowners prefer to reside in communities that are more segregated by their race rather than in neighborhoods with better circumstances inhabited by other races. In this regard, it is possible to argue that racial factors are more influential than socioeconomic reasons (Alba et al., 2000).

There are numerous political and historical causes for residential segregation based on racial preferences, all of which can be categorized as group prejudice. An extensive body of research exists on ways to make neighborhoods more inclusive. However, this paper does not elaborate on group prejudice's causes and proposed solutions. My goal is to examine the influence of these communities and the houses there on living circumstances, regardless of how individuals and families choose where to live. According to this perspective, studies indicate that housing costs considerably impact residential segregation in California.

This finding compels us to concentrate on the third factor for residential segregation: housing discrimination. Although California does not have legal housing discrimination based on race, housing restrictions significantly contribute to the state's ethnoracial segregation by driving up household prices much above the national average. Although minority groups prefer to live with members of their own ethnicity, it does not imply that they choose to live in unstable and dangerous neighborhoods. Nonetheless, due to artificial and de facto segregative housing regulations, Hispanics and African Americans have fewer housing options.

Before considering how California housing restrictions have worsened residential segregation and living conditions for low-income households, it is important to examine the current state of segregation in a study on Los Angeles, providing a clearer understanding of the problem's scope. Research conducted in 2016 by the UCLA Center for Neighborhood Knowledge analyzed the evolution of residential segregation between 1970 and 2014 in Los Angeles County. According to the study's overall findings, segregation between Blacks and Whites remained the highest compared to other group comparisons. However, Black-White segregation is decreasing, albeit slowly. In contrast, Hispanics are increasingly segregated from other ethnoracial populations. Compared to Blacks and Hispanics, the Asian population is the least segregated. Approximately three-quarters of Los Angeles is dominated by a single ethnoracial group (Paul et al., 2016).

The disparity index (DI) made for the report ranges the neighborhoods from 0.0 (complete integration) to 1.0 (complete segregation). "DI is the percent of a population that would have to move from areas where it is concentrated to less concentrated places in order to achieve full integration. For example, if the DI for Blacks and Whites is .50, then half of the Blacks (or Whites) would have to relocate to achieve integration" (Paul et al., 2016, p. 12).

Table 4

Household Dissimilarity Indices

	1970	1980	1990	2000	2014
Black-White	89.7	79.3	72.4	68.9	66.4
Hispanic-White	60.9	54.5	57.3	60.6	60.1
Asian-White	52.1	46.6	46.2	49.2	48.6
Asian-Black	76.5	74.0	68.6	68.4	66.2
Black-Hispanic	60.0	46.7	47.0	53.2	53.0

After reaching its peak in the 1970s, Black-White neighborhood segregation has steadily declined, as shown in the table above. However, since the 1990s, there has been no major advancement in Black-White integration. Since the 1980s, Hispanic-White neighborhood segregation has increased, and among the major communities, Asians are the least segregated ethnoracial group (Paul et al., 2016).

The study also drew conclusions based on the neighborhood's changing demographics. In 1970, 89% of Whites resided in neighborhoods where more than 70% of residents were White. By 2014, this percentage had plummeted to 37%. In the 1970s, 69% of Blacks lived in neighborhoods with more than 70% Black residents. However, in 2014, only 16% of Blacks did. In contrast, in 2014, 59% of Hispanics lived in communities that were

70% Hispanic, compared to 28% in 1970. Nonetheless, Whites are the most segregated group since 67% of Whites continue to reside in majority-White communities (Paul et al., 2016).

The Terner Center for Housing Innovation's 2019 analysis indicated that house prices climbed in California neighborhoods with rigorous housing regulations while most locals opposed new construction (Kneebone & Trainer, 2019). Whites and white-collar employees predominate in neighborhoods with tight anti-density zoning regulations. In contrast, Hispanics and Blacks are the majority in neighborhoods where multifamily housing is permitted and rigorous housing rules do not exist. In addition, most Hispanics and Blacks in these neighborhoods hold low-income blue-collar employment and support the establishment of new settlements in their communities.

It is natural for people and families to prioritize where and with whom they would like to reside. However, California's single-housing rules and anti-density zoning policies prevent the effective use of land, causing house prices and rents to surge much above the national average. In addition to racial factors, low-income families are restricted to certain neighborhoods. Moreover, as housing prices and rents continue to rise, blue-collar employees' real wages continue to decline. As the population density in neighborhoods of multifamily housing rises, environmental conditions continue to deteriorate. Homeowners in single-family neighborhoods raise the value of their properties while actively preventing their environmental deterioration.

I do not know how racially diverse California's neighborhoods would have been without the state's stringent housing laws. However, the cost of these stringent housing laws to the low-income population is quantifiable. In Los Angeles, jurisdictions with strict lot size regulations have 32% higher rents and 38% higher housing prices than jurisdictions with comparatively moderate lot size standards. Moreover, the price differential between rent and house values in San Francisco is 36% and 54%, respectively. In San Jose, rents are essentially identical across zoning regimes, although property prices in areas with big minimum lot sizes are 78% higher (Rothwell, 2019). This study found that minimum lot size restrictions reliably and consistently predict higher housing costs and larger houses, with an 8% increase in rents and housing values for each standard deviation increase in minimum lot size requirements (Rothwell, 2019).

These numbers illustrate the socioeconomic dimension of California's residential segregation. Citizen opposition to residential buildings is stronger in more educated jurisdictions, implying that projects that meet the neighborhood's legal standards are delayed (Rothwell, 2019). Anti-multifamily zoning jurisdictions are more racially segregated. In jurisdictions where land is primarily allocated to single-family detached housing, the proportion of Black and Hispanic residents in the metropolitan area is significantly lower (Rothwell, 2019). According to the report, the proportion of land zoned for single-family detached housing predicts a lower proportion of Black and Hispanic residents and a higher proportion of Whites. Minimum lot sizes predict lower Hispanic population shares, but they do not affect Black population shares (Rothwell, 2019). There is also compelling evidence that the proportion of land zoned for single-family use and minimum lot size restrictions dramatically estimates lower proportions of blue-collar workers (Rothwell, 2019).

Crime and Residential Segregation

No one prefers living in neighborhoods with poorer circumstances, but ethnoracial communities are more likely to reside in neighborhoods where they are the majority. However, increased housing costs result in poorer and more disadvantaged communities. Ethnic populations with low incomes predominantly inhabit these communities in California.

The violent crime rate tends to be higher in neighborhoods where disadvantage is prevalent. Numerous studies have repeatedly demonstrated that neighborhoods with greater income inequality have higher crime rates. Even in cities such as Stockholm, which are relatively safe and have low-income disparity, the murder rate in impoverished districts is significantly higher than in other parts of the city (U.S. Department of Housing and

Urban Development, 2016). In California, crime sites are synonymous with similarly impoverished neighborhoods.

In addition to income disparity, racially segregated neighborhoods are more vulnerable to violent crime. However, several studies underline that the spillover effect on nearby communities of neighborhoods with a high crime rate happens regardless of the ethnic composition of the neighborhoods. In this regard, the high crime rates in the city are directly tied to residential segregation, and criminal activity is not restricted to particular neighborhoods. Therefore, it is plausible to assert that residential segregation negatively impacts the city (Krivo et al., 2009).

Disruption of social cohesion is the most significant social problem created by residential segregation and income inequality in neighborhoods. If residents in a neighborhood lack trust in one another, they will be less eager to work for the common good. Therefore, low social cohesion facilitates the rise in neighborhood crime rates. According to numerous studies, young people in neighborhoods with low social trust and cohesion may be more prone to commit crimes if they believe they are left to deal with their problems alone.

Examining the racial distribution of California's incarceration rates reveals a stark disparity across the races (The Sentencing Project, 2019):

- White imprisonment rate per 100,000: 175 (39th-highest among all states)

- Black imprisonment rate per 100,000: 1,623 (14th-highest among all states)
- Black to White ratio: 9.3
- Hispanic imprisonment rate per 100,000: 353 (17th-highest among all states)
- Hispanic to White ratio: 2.0

Certainly, high housing costs are not directly responsible for the distribution of incarceration rates by race seen above. However, it is impossible to remark on the necessary social policies in California without considering the interconnected and complex character of social problems. We must not forget the influence of the butterfly effect on social issues. However, if we take a more optimistic view of the matter, the positive consequences of strong social policies that result in structural changes may exceed our expectations. In this regard, housing costs are crucial to stabilizing California's neighborhoods. California's housing expenses are more political than economic. Therefore, a lack of political will, not effective economic measures, is preventing the resolution of these issues.

Studying the homeless population in California is one approach to observing the butterfly effect caused by California's housing problem on the streets. Although homelessness is associated with mental health issues and drug addiction, housing costs directly cause homelessness in California. There are 130,000 homeless people throughout the state. Approximately 28,000 homeless individuals reside in the San Francisco Bay area, whereas 60,000 reside in Los Angeles County. Santa Barbara, with a population of 91,847, is believed to have more than 1,800 homeless people. One of every 50 individuals in Santa Barbara is homeless. Alarmingly, California is home to half of the homeless population in the US (Tanner, 2021).

The problem of homelessness in California is a social crisis in its own right, and mental illness or substance abuse cannot be used to explain its origin. The fundamental cause of homelessness is the lack of affordable housing options for low-income persons. It is quite probable that job losses, medical issues, and family issues will result in the loss of income for individuals, and income losses will result in eviction and homelessness. According to studies, one-third of the homeless population in Los Angeles is a result of economic losses (Tanner, 2021).

It is extremely challenging to reintegrate a homeless individual into society. The attitude of the police and the general public toward the homeless strongly favors their continued homelessness. People who are homeless often wind up in jail. Approximately 5% of San Francisco's homeless spend the night in jail. Within a year, at least half of the homeless were incarcerated (Tanner, 2021). Decidedly, incarceration does not improve mental health or help you get a job.

There is also a significant connection between homelessness or housing insecurity and employment opportunities. For instance, a study conducted in Milwaukee between 2009 and 2011 found that people who involuntarily lost their homes were 20% more likely to lose their jobs than those with comparable jobs who did not lose their homes (Desmond & Gershenson, 2016). Therefore, it is simple to show a connection between persistent unemployment and crime rates or list parental incarceration's detrimental impacts on children.

Not only the homeless face the risk of incarceration. In the US, the phenomenon of mass incarceration has evolved into a distinct socioeconomic crisis. Although mass incarceration has little effect on crime rates or rehabilitation, it has catastrophic consequences on individuals and their families. Those who transgress the law are unquestionably required by justice to be punished. However, governments and communities can modify the conditions that encourage criminal behavior.

According to research by Villanova University, mass incarceration worsens poverty by 20% in the US. The rise in poverty is not attributable to the inability of prisoners to be economically productive. However, incarceration's negative impacts on families, particularly children, are most concerning. For instance, studies have found that when a father goes to prison, there is a 40% chance that his family will be poor. In 2016, approximately 1.5 million dads with children were incarcerated at the state or federal level. Black and Hispanic children are two to seven times more likely than White children to have incarcerated fathers.

There are further intriguing statistics. A 14-year-old Black youngster whose father lacks a high school diploma has an approximately 50/50 risk of going to jail (Tanner, 2021). It should come as no surprise to anyone that children whose fathers are in prison at significant times in their lives develop anti-social behavior, are prone to crime, or drop out of school.

Studies indicate that the likelihood of a family falling into poverty increases by 38% when the father is incarcerated. Upon release from prison, a person's income typically declines by roughly 40%. According to a Pew Charitable Trusts survey, released prisoners from 1986 remained in the bottom 20% of income earners in 2006. A 2003 poll revealed that 65% of incarcerated individuals did not complete high school, and 14% had education below the eighth grade. In comparison, we might anticipate that the social difficulties of educated and financially secure individuals would lead them to commit less serious crimes (Pew Charitable Trusts, 2016).

A study evaluating the association between violent crime and residential instability in Los Angeles between 1992 and 1997 revealed that violent crime promotes residential instability regardless of racial or ethnic composition. According to the study, a 1% increase in violent crime correlates to a 1.5% increase in the volume of homes sold in an average area. This ratio most likely reflects the desire of residents to leave neighborhoods with a high violent crime rate and move to safer neighborhoods (Boggess & Hipp, 2010).

However, no substantial correlation was discovered between house turnover and crime rates. For example, no correlation was observed between home sales and crime rates in Los Angeles. According to the report, poorer residents may not have the financial flexibility to relocate neighborhoods in response to increased crime rates. However, low levels of instability diminish violent crime rates in Latino-dominated communities. In contrast, when residential instability rises, there is a rapid surge in violent crime rates (Boggess & Hipp, 2010).

Black communities in Los Angeles are another intriguing conclusion of the study since residential stability does not diminish the violent crime rate in mostly Black communities. Conversely, residential stability, assessed in terms of tenants, has increased violent crime rates. As stated previously, Blacks have a strong propensity to live in mostly Black communities. However, if low-income Blacks do not have access to safer neighborhoods with lower rents, they remain in their communities despite increased crime rates (Boggess & Hipp, 2010).

Another study demonstrated that vacancies and evictions might raise the crime rate by destabilizing neighborhoods. Vacant properties enhance the rate of criminal activity. According to a 2016 study in Milwaukee, evictions hinder the formation of social cohesion by interrupting the relationships between neighborhood inhabitants. As a result, neighborhood residents cannot establish crime-prevention practices (Pew Charitable Trusts, 2016).

Families transferring to less impoverished neighborhoods with the assistance of housing vouchers have exhibited extremely favorable trends, as explained in detail when addressing the problem of schooling. For instance, the health of parents and children has improved, while the prevalence of adolescent female obesity has declined. Individuals in more dangerous neighborhoods experience greater stress because they are afraid to leave their homes, and stress increases obesity (Fish et al., 2010).

Numerous instances of such negative outcomes might be cited. In neighborhoods of concentrated poverty and disadvantage, sexual harassment, exploitation, and violence against women and girls can become acceptable in coercive sexual circumstances. Again, as may be easily surmised, these poor environmental conditions have a greater impact on the sexual development of young girls living in impoverished ethnoracial communities. Hence, teenage girls are more likely to experience long-term psychological stress and substance abuse (Popkin et al., 2015).

Another study conducted in the 2000s in Chicago looked at children's exposure to neighborhood violence over time and discovered that, after controlling for differences between students, children living in more violent neighborhoods fall further behind their peers in school as they get older and that the magnitude of this effect is comparable to that of socioeconomic disadvantage (Burdick-Will, 2016). On a broader level, Chetty and Hendren (2018) discovered that children who grow up in high-crime neighborhoods face huge economic losses as adults.

Education Trapped by High Housing Costs

There are two negative effects of high housing costs on children's schooling. First, school achievement in underserved neighborhoods is worse than in less impoverished neighborhoods. Second, when families regularly move neighborhoods because they cannot afford the rent or unfavorable neighborhood conditions, students must frequently change schools.

Multiple factors contribute to the low performance of schools in poor communities compared to those in less impoverished neighborhoods. Schools in disadvantaged neighborhoods receive fewer financial resources than schools in wealthier neighborhoods. While this is somewhat true because school fees have historically been related to property taxes, California's school funding reforms have substantially resolved this issue. However, the performance problem of schools in low-income communities persists.

The two most essential elements shaping the quality of education, besides finances, can be defined. First, it is possible to illustrate the parents' social capital and their time on their children's education. Children's intellectual and academic development is strongly influenced by the knowledge and behaviors they acquire from their social surroundings. The less and poorer the intellectual input is, the greater the possibility that children will be less inclined toward intellectual issues.

The cumulative impacts of the social environment under the influence of peers in schools can also be noticed. Studies have determined the significant influence of children from similar socioeconomic strata on each other's academic development. Indeed, the academic achievement of students younger than 13 who attend schools in less impoverished neighborhoods than schools in impoverished neighborhoods is much higher.

Second, students with housing insecurity are likely to switch neighborhoods and schools more frequently than their peers. Changes in the neighborhood and school might make it difficult for students to adapt to school and reduce academic achievement. In California, the dropout rate for socioeconomically disadvantaged students is 21.3%, while this rate is 17.5% statewide (California Department of Housing and Community Development, 2013). The American Housing Survey indicated that 55% of children from low-income families move annually, and less than one-third of non-low-income households' children have moved annually. Families spending more than 50% of their income on housing are more likely to relocate than those paying less (Tanner, 2021).

Figure 5

Percentage of Children Who Moved From 2007–2009 by Income Group

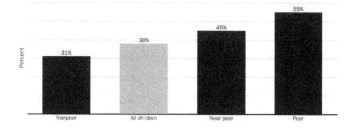

Source: From Rebecca Cohen and Keith Wardrip, "Should I Stay or Should I Go? Exploring the Effects of Housing Mobility on Children," Center for Housing Policy, February 2011.

On the standard reading test administered to Minnesota first- through sixth-graders, pupils who switched homes and schools three or more times scored 20 points worse than those who did not change homes (Cohen & Wardrip, 2011). The 2005 American Housing Survey also included information regarding the relationship between mobility and poor housing conditions. Families unable to pay their electricity bill, rent, or mortgage in the previous 12 months were substantially more likely to relocate than other families. Loss of a housing subsidy significantly impacts the likelihood of relocation (Cohen & Wardrip, 2011). Those who are dissatisfied with the quality of their neighborhood move more frequently than those who are satisfied (Cohen & Wardrip, 2011). Low-income families may become trapped in a hopeless migration due to a dreadful neighborhood environment. Moreover, it is highly improbable that the new homes these families would inhabit will be better than their former residences.

In the US, we can analyze a significant experiment on the long-term consequences of the neighborhood on children's lives. The US Department of Housing and Urban Development developed the Moving to Opportunity (MTO) initiative in five major cities between 1994 and 1998. The primary objective of the MTO was to provide housing vouchers to randomly selected families from high-poverty districts so that they might relocate to less-poverty districts and to monitor the socioeconomic changes associated with these families. One of the most crucial considerations was whether economic gaps would reduce as families moved to less impoverished communities.

In total, 4,604 families participated in MTO. Some families were granted housing vouchers on the condition that they relocate to a neighborhood with a poverty rate of less than 10%. The second group of families received subsidized standard housing with no conditions attached. In contrast, the remaining families in the control group did not receive housing aid other than public housing. This extensive study examined the short-term, medium-term, and long-term effects of moving to wealthier communities (Chetty et al., 2016).

According to MTO's short- and medium-term research, moving to less impoverished neighborhoods improves mental health, physical health, and family safety (Katz et al., 2001). However, these researchers showed that MTO had little influence on young adults' wages or employment rates. Therefore, the relevant studies have indicated no correlation between neighborhood environment and economic success.

After 2010, R. Chetty reevaluated the MTO experience of N. Hendren and L. Katz. Midway through the 1990s, monitoring and evaluating the socioeconomic positions of children who transferred communities within the program's reach as adults became feasible. Children under the age of 13 who moved to less impoverished neighborhoods were more likely to attend college and much more likely to achieve better salaries, the most startling finding of the study.

These children reside in better communities as adults and are less likely to be single parents. They can even positively influence the lives of their grandchildren. However, while there is no evidence for these good prospects for children older than 13 years, it has been found that in some instances, older children are severely impacted by a change in neighborhoods. Furthermore, the study demonstrated that girls under 13 do better than boys under 13. This insightful study demonstrated that integrating disadvantaged families into mixed-income neighborhoods contributes to positively reducing intergenerational poverty (Chetty et al., 2016).

A large-scale social experiment demonstrated that the socioeconomic condition of students' schoolmates significantly impacts their academic performance. R. Ewijk and P. Sleegers undertook a meta-analysis of empirical studies on the topic through 2010, which largely supported peer-effect hypotheses (Van Ewijk & Sleegers, 2010). Comparisons between schools attended by low-income students and other schools on national standardized examinations also demonstrated this phenomenon. For example, only 18% of students from low-income homes scored "proficient" on academic achievement assessments, compared to approximately 48% of the rest of the student population. However, in schools with a high proportion of low-income kids, just 7.4% of students score "proficient"—less than half as many (Tanner, 2021).

We cannot level all students' socioeconomic status. In any case, this political endeavor is neither desirable nor attainable. However, removing the barriers placed artificially before students and families is possible. In California, the absence of affordable housing is one of the most significant variables affecting the academic success of low-income students. However, initiatives that cut housing costs have an enormously favorable influence on students' future expectations.

Conclusion

As demonstrated in this chapter, housing insecurity and residential segregation are complex social phenomena with lasting effects. Without a complete examination of the historical, cultural, and economic elements, it is impossible to remark on residential segregation and its effects. However, scientific investigations have demonstrated that high housing costs negatively affect the environmental conditions of segregated neighborhoods. Therefore, we may investigate the social crises caused by housing finance in segregated neighborhoods by separating it from other segregation-related issues.

There are two primary ways in which housing costs impact the lives of individuals and families. First, housing expenses aggravate conditions in neighborhoods already severely separated. Although housing costs are not the primary cause of segregation, unaffordable property prices and rents are the primary sources of deteriorating environmental conditions in the neighborhoods of minority communities. The financial and psychological strain imposed on low-income families by artificially rising property prices in California due to ineffective regulations has far-reaching spillover effects. The segregation crisis, which has long-term effects, cannot be resolved fast, but there are rapid and readily implemented solutions that can reduce the high housing costs that exacerbate this social crisis.

Second, excessively inflated property prices are widening the gap between segregated neighborhoods. It entails the removal of Black and Hispanic families from communities dominated by Whites, particularly in California. Although segregation can be partially based on families' preferences, the financial status of families who wish to escape the conditions of their neighborhood may force them to remain there. Since segregated families cannot actively improve their family members' living conditions, they pass on the detrimental consequences of environmental conditions to the following generation. This inheritance produces a vicious cycle where the harmful social problems associated with segregation are passed on to the following generation, becoming chronic and even worsening.

Perhaps a third option should be added to the above two. As ethnoracial neighborhoods in California become more divided, advantaged high-income groups rely on their housing privileges even more. In privileged neighborhoods, the perception that the phenomena of high crime and poverty in segregated communities result from individual character traits would ultimately gain momentum. A protective impulse promotes the exclusionary boundary between advantaged and disadvantaged groups. This exclusionary attitude is especially visible in the treatment of homeless Californians. Most privileged Californians' approach to the problem of homelessness is restricted to diminishing the exposure of the homeless in public spaces. These policy suggestions resemble burying our heads in the sand like an ostrich.

The opposition of privileged neighborhoods to loosening housing rules in their communities is another example of an exclusive attitude. There are economic reasons for this viewpoint. Economically, increasing the number of houses in a neighborhood will decrease housing prices. Landlords do not desire this effect. In addition, as the number of luxury properties has reduced, middle- and upper-income groups now need to relocate and pay more for housing to enjoy the same neighborhood characteristics. As previously explained, many social problems resulting from segregation and housing insecurity can be shaped independently of individual preferences. These environmental implications necessitate the development of profound policies. The problems caused by segregation will begin to have spillover consequences that will also harm advantageous neighborhoods. These spillover consequences of segregation cannot be eliminated by affluent neighborhoods raising their invisible borders.

The construction of affordable housing in California is achievable and a civic necessity. The first step is to reduce the housing industry's stringent limitations and regulations. Then, through expanding housing voucher options, families living in socially segregated communities should be given a chance to reside in communities with better environmental circumstances. These proposed solutions will have positive short-term effects, particularly for residents of neighborhoods with unstable environments. However, long term, the winner will be the entire state of California, including its affluent communities.

References

Alba, R. D., Logan, J. R., & Stults, B. J. (2000). How segregated are middle-class African Americans? *Social Problems, 47*(4), 543–558. https://doi.org/10.2307/3097134

Boggess, L. N., & Hipp, J. R. (2010). Violent crime, residential instability and mobility: Does the relationship differ in minority neighborhoods? *Journal of Quantitative Criminology, 26*(3), 351–370.

Burdick-Will, J. (2016). Neighborhood violent crime and academic growth in Chicago: Lasting effects of early exposure. *Social Forces, 95*(1), 133–158. https://doi.org/10.1093/sf/sow041

California Department of Housing and Community Development. (2013). *Housing and educational attainment* [Report]. https://www.hcd.ca.gov/policy-research/plans-reports/docs/pb03housing_education0214.pdf

Chetty, R., & Hendren, N. (2018). The impacts of neighborhoods on intergenerational mobility I: Childhood exposure effects. *The Quarterly Journal of Economics, 133*(3), 1107–1162. https://doi.org/10.1093/qje/qjy007

Chetty, R., Hendren, N., & Katz, L. F. (2016). The effects of exposure to better neighborhoods on children: New evidence from the Moving to Opportunity experiment. *American Economic Review, 106*(4), 855–902. https://doi.org/10.1257/aer.20150572

Cohen, R., & Wardrip, K. (2011). *Should I stay or should I go?: Exploring the effects of housing instability and mobility on children* [Report]. Center for Housing Policy. https://mcstudy.norc.org/publications/files/CohenandWardrip_2009.pdf

Desmond, M., & Gershenson, C. (2016). Housing and employment insecurity among the working poor. *Social Problems*, *63*(1), 46–67. https://doi.org/10.1093/socpro/spv025

Family Promise of Southern Ocean County. (2021, January 27). What is housing insecurity? *Family Promise Blog*. https://www.familypromisesoc.org/post/what-is-housing-insecurity

Fernández-Villaverde, J., & Ohanian, L. (2018). Housing policy reform. In S. W. Atlas, J. Fernández-Villaverde, E. Hanushek, E. P. Lazear, L. Ohanian, J. D. Rauh, & F. A. Wolak (Eds.), *Economic policy challenges facing California's next governor* (pp. 15–18). Hoover Institution. https://www.hoover.org/sites/default/files/research/docs/economicpolicychallengescalifornia_ohanian_hooverinstitution_10-2018_updated.pdf

Fish, J. S., Ettner, S., Ang, A., & Brown, A. F. (2010). Association of perceived neighborhood safety on body mass index. *American Journal of Public Health*, *100*(11), 2296–2303. https://doi.org/10.2105/AJPH.2009.183293

Fox, L. E., & Burns, K. (2021). *The Supplemental Poverty Measure: 2020* (Report No. P60-275). U.S. Census Bureau. https://www.census.gov/content/dam/Census/library/publications/2021/demo/p60-275.pdf

Healthy People. (2022). *Housing instability*. Retrieved August 19, 2022, from https://www.healthypeople.gov/2020/topics-objectives/topic/social-determinants-health/interventions-resources/housing-instability

Johnson, H., Lafortune, J., & Mejia, M. (2020). *California's future: Housing*. Public Policy Institute of California. https://eric.ed.gov/?q=source%3A%22Policy+Futures+in+Education&ff1=autJohnson%2C+Hans&id=ED603736

Katz, L. F., Kling, J. R., & Liebman, J. B. (2001). Moving to opportunity in Boston: Early results of a randomized mobility experiment. *The Quarterly Journal of Economics*, *116*(2), 607–654. https://doi.org/10.1162/00335530151144113

Kneebone, E., & Trainer, M. (2019). *How housing supply shapes access to entry-level homeownership* [Report]. Terner Center for Housing Innovation. https://ternercenter.berkeley.edu/wp-content/uploads/pdfs/How_Housing_Supply_Shapes_Access_to_Entry-Level_Homeownership_2019.pdf

Krivo, L. J., Peterson, R. D., & Kuhl, D. C. (2009). Segregation, racial structure, and neighborhood violent crime. *American Journal of Sociology*, *114*(6), 1765–1802. https://doi.org/10.1086/597285

Leopold, J., Cunningham, M., Posey, L., & Manuel, T. (2022). *Improving measures of housing insecurity: A path forward*. Urban Institute. https://www.urban.org/sites/default/files/publication/101608/improving_measures_of_housing_insecurity.pdf

National Low Income Housing Coalition. (n.d.). *Housing needs by state: California*. Retrieved August 18. 2022, from https://nlihc.org/housing-needs-by-state/california

Ong, P., Pech, C., Chhea, J., & Lee, C. A. (2016). *Race, ethnicity, and income segregation in Los Angeles* [Report]. UCLA Center for Neighborhood Knowledge. https://knowledge.luskin.ucla.edu/wp-content/uploads/2018/01/Race-Ethnicity-and-Income-Segregation-Ziman_2016.pdf

Pew Charitable Trusts. (2016). *Household expenditures and income: Balancing family finances in today's economy* [Report]. https://www.pewtrusts.org/en/research-and-analysis/issue-briefs/2016/03/household-expenditures-and-income

Popkin, S. J., Bogle, M., Zweig, J. M., Saxena, P., Breslav, L., & Michie, M. (2015). *Let girls be girls: How coercive sexual environments affect girls who live in disadvantaged communities and what we can do about it* [Report]. Urban Institute. https://www.urban.org/sites/default/files/publication/72466/2000490-Let-Girls-Be-Girls.pdf

Rothwell, J. (2019, September 5). *Land use politics, housing costs, and segregation in California cities.* Terner Center for Housing Innovation. https://ternercenter.berkeley.edu/research-and-policy/land-use-politics-housing-costs-and-segregation-in-california-cities/

The Sentencing Project. (2019). *State by state data.* Retrieved from https://www.sentencingproject.org/thefacts/#detail?state1Option=California&state2Option=0

Tanner, M. D. (2021). *Cato's project on poverty and inequality in California: Final report.* Cato Institute. https://www.cato.org/sites/cato.org/files/2021-10/California Project Final Report.pdf

U.S. Census Bureau. (2018). *American Community Survey: B25031: Median gross rent by bedrooms.* https://data.census.gov/cedsci/table?q=median rent californai&tid=ACSDT1Y2018.B25031

U.S. Census Bureau. (2021). *Poverty thresholds.* Retrieved from https://www.census.gov/data/tables/time-series/demo/income-poverty/historical-povertythresholds.html

U.S. Department of Housing and Urban Development. (2016). *Neighborhoods and violent crime.* https://www.huduser.gov/portal/periodicals/em/summer16/highlight2.html

Van Ewijk, R., & Sleegers, P. (2010). Peer ethnicity and achievement: A meta-analysis into the compositional effect. *School Effectiveness and School Improvement, 21*(3), 237–265. https://doi.org/10.1080/09243451003612671

Williams, D. R., & Collins, C. (2001). Racial residential segregation: A fundamental cause of racial disparities in health. *Public Health Reports, 116*(5), 404–416. https://www.ncbi.nlm.nih.gov/pmc/articles/PMC1497358

Woetzel, J., Mischke, J., Peloquin, S., & Weisfield, D. (2016). *A tool kit to close California's housing gap: 3.5 million homes by 2025* [Report]. McKinsey & Company. https://www.mckinsey.com/~/media/McKinsey/Industries/Public and Social Sector/Our Insights/Closing Californias housing gap/Closing-Californias-housing-gap-Full-report.pdf

World Population Review. (2022). *Average rent by state 2022.* Retrieved August 19, 2022, from https://worldpopulationreview.com/state-rankings/average-rent-by-state

About the Author

D r. Rodgir Cohen is a university lecturer. As a combat veteran, Rodgir strongly believes in restoring governmental power to the grassroots level. He holds the values of justice and equality for all people as guiding principles when teaching. His current hobbies include boating and roasting coffee. Rodgir resides in Redlands, California, with his wife and three children.